CONFIDENT PARENTING
IN
CHALLENGING TIMES

Essential Convictions of
Highly Successful Parents

CONFIDENT PARENTING
IN
CHALLENGING TIMES

Essential Convictions of
Highly Successful Parents

RICHARD PATTERSON, JR.

TEKNA BOOKS
Chanhassen, Minnesota

CONFIDENT PARENTING IN CHALLENGING TIMES
Essential Convictions of Highly Successful Parents

Publisher's Cataloging-in-Publication
(Provided by Quality Books, Inc.)

Patterson, Richard, 1948-
    Confident parenting in challenging times :
essential convictions of highly successful parents
/ Richard Patterson, Jr. -- 1st ed.
    p. cm.
    Includes bibliographical references and index.
    LCCN: 99-60658
    ISBN: 0-9664413-3-8

    1. Parenting--United States. 2. Parenting--
Religious aspects. 3. Child rearing. I. Title.

HQ769.P38 1999   649.1
                            QBI99-285

Published by **TEKNA BOOKS™**
www.teknabooks.com

Printed in the USA by Morris Publishing
3212 East Hwy 30, Kearney, NE 68847
1-800-650-7888

1   2   3   4   5   99   00   01   02   03

To the Parent from whom every family in heaven and on earth takes its name.

Soli Deo Gloria

CONTENTS

Introduction

Becoming a Highly Successful Parent!

Oprah Winfrey is the host of a highly successful TV talk show, an actress, and successful businesswoman. She is clearly self-confident and accomplished. But all her success has not given her confidence to be a successful parent. When asked why she was not planning to marry and have children soon, she replied, "I'm afraid that I will not be able to live up to what I believe a mother should be. I would be afraid that I would make a lot of the mistakes my mother made with me."[1]

Many parents today feel like Oprah Winfrey. They're unsure of themselves, unable to trust their own judgement, and unable to act confidently on behalf of their children's best interests. Over and over during my years of observing and training parents, I've seen them acting with fear and hesitancy. In the supermarket, they're afraid to set a limit on how many snacks their child can have while shopping. They send an obviously sick five-year-old to school "because she said she wants to go" when they know she should be at home in bed. They hesitate to set healthy limits on their teenager's dating patterns, fearing that their child will "hate" them.

They certainly want to be effective and successful parents but fear, guilt, and a sense of inadequacy get in the way. And it's no wonder! Parenting has become a complex and complicated endeavor in our society. It isn't easy at all. In fact, the prospect of being a parent can be downright frightening!

Being a successful parent today is a lot like running a marathon. It's a significant challenge that requires major amounts of discipline and endurance. And those who finish successfully are the ones who keep on running, determined and confident, all the way to the end of the course.

But becoming a highly successful parent requires even more than running a marathon! In fact, some quite intimidating challenges face parents today. Technology such as television and computers opens a complex, confusing, and sometimes threatening world to preschoolers. Conflicting and constantly changing moral values confront and confound adolescents. Fluctuating social norms and family forms make all of us unsure of what is really true and reliable.

These challenges add to parents' insecurities in their search for a steady and sure foundation on which to build their families. They're burdened by a nagging suspicion that, if they had to pass a test in order to become parents, they might not make the grade.

If you're not careful, you can get discouraged—even question why anyone would want to bring children into this world. But once you do have children, and you feel yourself giving and receiving the deep and unconditional love that flows between parent and child, you know it's good—very, very good—to be a parent, challenges and all. The problems, pain, and disappointments of parenting must be faced, but they can never still the voice within us that says, "I **will** be a good parent to my child, the best parent I can be. My love demands it and my child deserves nothing less."

So from the day our baby is born, we resolve to be the very best possible parents our child could have. If they rated parents, our goal would be to merit a rating of not just "good" or even "successful," but "excellent" or "highly successful." We persevere through years of diapers, dishes, discipline, and driving lessons, sustained by the hope that, in the end, our children will turn out to be stable, responsible, moral, and productive adults.

Is It Really Possible?

Is it just a "vain hope," or is it really possible to be a highly successful parent today? The "experts" certainly think so. They bombard us with all kinds of advice from many different perspectives. They'll tell us anything from how often to pick up a crying infant to how to talk so our teens won't just tune us out. And anytime you get two parenting experts in a room, you get three different opinions. So whom do you trust?

Asking—and answering—that question is how highly successful parenting begins. You see, it's not just "experts" who believe that you and I can be successful parents (with lots of help from them, of course!). During twenty-five years of speaking around this country, I've met thousands of parents who believe it, too. They know it's true because they're doing it every day. They've told me their stories, their insights and experiences, and the wisdom they've gained. I've distilled them into this book of essential convictions that guide everything they do, including every parenting decision they make. I share those with you in the pages that follow.

I promise you that I won't share with you anything I don't believe in myself. We parents don't need any more nice sounding but impractical theories. And as a parent for nearly a quarter-century, I'm convinced that the parents I've spoken with across the country are right—we can be happy and highly successful parents. By the time you've finished this book, I think you'll be convinced of it, too.

11

Holding onto that conviction is the foundation of successful parenting. Highly successful parents don't love their children more or less than any other parents but their love is more than just a strong "feeling" or affirmation. Like reinforced steel, it's infused and strengthened by foundational convictions that serve to both guard and guide that love. It is this set of convictions that enables successful parents to steer a steady course through the confusing waters of conflicting values and "expert" voices. These essential convictions enable these parents to keep a steady hand on the rudder of the family "ship" as they navigate the shoals, sandbars, storms, and dangers on the voyage toward their goal.

The highly successful parent knows all too well that she is not perfect—not by any definition! But no expert, no matter how wise or committed, can love or understand your child like you do. God gave your child to you and you to your child. He put you together for His good and gracious purposes. And together, you can realize them.

The Best Parent My Child Could Have

So the first and most fundamental conviction held by highly successful parents is this: *"I may not be perfect, but I (and no one else) am the best parent my child could have."* This conviction gives us confidence to follow our parenting instincts as we journey along the complicated roads of parenting. It allows us to arrive at our destination with the pride and satisfaction we long for—and deserve—as we launch our children into adulthood. When the difficult times shake them, highly successful parents remind themselves: "I am the best parent my child could have. I **am** a successful parent."

Highly successful parents are indeed confident, but they also realize they aren't perfect and that they don't have to be. They understand that parenting mistakes, like all failures, are opportunities for growth and learning. Common sense tells us that human children were designed by the Creator to be raised by human (that is, imperfect) parents. So highly successful parents don't let fear of failure stop them from following their instincts and doing what they think is best for their children. Experts can be helpful on occasion, but in the end, successful parents rely on their own "sanctified common sense" (common sense informed by the spiritual values they hold) to get the job done. Those are the issues we discuss in Chapters 1 and 2.

Highly successful parents recognize that, "For better or worse, no one will have a greater influence on my child than I, their parent, will." No other adult or expert shapes a child's life and spirit as deeply and fundamentally as their parent does. Successful parents realize that if they want their children to love and serve God and humanity, they, above everyone else, have it within their power to shape them in that direction. If they want their children to be responsible, productive, loving, and caring people, they, better than any other person, can show them the way.

Getting Our Act Together

It's no surprise that children resemble their parents. That's the way our bodies were designed. And it's no surprise, that, as they grow, we hear ourselves saying, "You sound just like your mother" or "That's just the way your father would act."

There's an old, common sense maxim that says that "the acorn doesn't fall far from the tree." Highly successful parents understand it well. They know their children are likely to grow up to be like them, so their parenting is guided by this second, common sense conviction: *"Good Parenting begins with Good Personing."* We can't give our children more than we have. We can't help them become more than we are (or are trying to become). We can't lead them where

13

we haven't been (or are headed). Successful parents are themselves growing mentally, emotionally, and spiritually, so they can give their best to their children. In Chapter 3, we examine the practical, every day implications of this conviction and look at some ways we can help our children grow in the direction we hope for them. It isn't all just wishing, "hit and miss," or chance. There are concrete, manageable things successful parents can do!

As complicated as parenting is today, it's no wonder we look for all the help we can get. It seems like too much responsibility for any one person! And, in fact, it is! Perhaps that's one reason why God gave children two parents! When one is weary, the other can be strong. When one is puzzled, the other understands. God said that it isn't good for humans to be alone, and parents do better together rather than alone, also.[2] It's just common sense that "two heads are better than one."

Highly successful parents understand that children need **both** of their parents. So they work at preserving and strengthening their marriages. That way, they'll both be there for their children. And when marriages do fail (or never take place to begin with), which parent usually fades from the life of the child? In most cases, it's the father.

Two Heads are Better!

Many single mothers are excellent parents whose children will one day certainly "rise up and call her blessed."[3] Yet children need—and deserve—fathers, also. Fathers have a special kind of love and a treasury of unique gifts to offer their children. So highly successful parents live by this third, simple common sense conviction also: *"Children are a two-parent project."* In Chapter 4, we'll discover some of the unique benefits that fathers give their children.

Realistic and Resourceful

As I speak to parents all around the country, I look into the eyes of hurried, harried and time-starved parents (and children!) desperately trying to be good spouses, good parents, good employees and good people. For them, life is a constant battle to balance competing demands for time. It's a constant struggle to set proper priorities. And we continually battle with the clock!

Our modern world of instant food, microwaves, faxes and e-mail makes it seem that everything can be done instantly! And it's true that some things can be done quickly—but not successful parenting. That takes time, and time together is the primary vehicle through which parents express their love to their children. Highly successful parents face the same time pressures as all parents, but one simple, common sense conviction helps them set their priorities for wisely using their time: *"Successful Parenting, Like Anything Worthwhile, Takes Time."* Highly successful parents know that while "fast" is okay for food, it does not work for parenting.

Highly successful parents are both realistic and resourceful in their stewardship of their time. In Chapter 5, we see some of the secrets they have discovered for making the most of the time they have, in order to pay the biggest dividends for the health and happiness of their families.

As the parent of two sons who are now grown, I can personally attest to how quickly family life and parenting days rush by! But I admit there were those times, when the children were young and our small, urban townhouse was filled with noise and the blur of their endless energy, it seemed our parenting days would stretch on forever!

Successful parents know that they only get one chance to parent their children. They know they need a "guiding principle," a basic precept which will keep them heading in the right direction as they make their daily parenting decisions. Sure, they love their children, but

15

somehow love isn't enough. They need a more concrete standard; one rooted both in the moral and spiritual values successful parents hold dear, and also in the practical demands of daily family life.

For highly successful parents that "guiding principle" and basic standard is the "Golden Rule": "Do unto others as you would have them do unto you."[4] Highly successful parents live by a conviction that is their own "Golden Rule of Parenting": *"I will treat my children at all times with the same love and respect with which I want to be treated."* In Chapter 6, we'll see how these parents apply the "Golden Rule" in everyday family life as well as the revolutionary difference that it makes.

My wife and I have been through most of the "discipline" challenges parents face: toilet training, homework, teen curfews, dating, driving, and all the other opportunities for teaching our children self-discipline. It has not always been easy to know and do the best thing for children who are constantly demanding more independence than seems safe or sane to grant them! But somehow, parenting has still been a very positive experience for us—even discipline.

That's another, perhaps surprising mark of highly successful parents. They have a positive approach to discipline. They understand that responsible, caring, productive and spiritually sensitive adults don't just "happen." They're raised to be that way by parents who understand that they're "apprenticing" children in the school of life and discipling them to become mature, responsible, caring adults. Though many tend to think of discipline primarily in negative terms ("behavior control," "spanking," "punishment"), highly successful parents understand that discipline is really a very positive, hopeful, and ultimately rewarding process closely related to "discipling," which, like "apprenticing," is another word for the process of training a child for life.

Accentuate the Positive

So, highly successful parents approach discipline in the family guided by the firm conviction that *"Discipline is really a very positive thing." In fact it's a process of "apprenticing" or "discipling" children in how to live a self-disciplined, spiritually, emotionally rich, and productive life."* Successful parents know that this involves verbal teaching, active modeling and demonstrating, as well as the use of consequences—both good and bad. That's the approach to discipline we discuss in Chapter 7. In Chapter 8, we then explore some other major, perhaps controversial tools of discipline—spanking and timeout—as well as practical guidelines for using them.

We've said that highly successful parents are realistic. They know that, in the end, their children will grow up and make their own choices. And at the point where parents have done their best, they can only give their children over to God. However, that realism, discussed in our closing chapter, is not cynical or without hope. For the final, fundamental conviction of all highly successful parents is this: *"There are no guarantees in life-except one: God is faithful."*

When their children leave port to navigate the oceans of life on their own, highly successful parents may be anxious, but never discouraged. They know that love never fails, hope is sure, prayer is effective, and God is faithful. They know that they have done their best, loved their children fiercely, and lived by their convictions. As they send their children out into the world, they do so with hope and confidence—in their efforts and in their children—but most of all in the one who loves their children perfectly—God.

Confidence. That is a hallmark of the thousands of highly successful parents I've met over the years. Where does this confidence come from? It grows from these seven deeply held convictions that guide them daily. As I've observed and talked with these successful parents, they've shared these convictions with me. Different parents might word them slightly differently, but they all would agree with the essential convictions given in the following pages. So, as they first shared them with me, now I share them with you—in the firm conviction that you, too, can be a highly successful parent!

Chapter 1

The Key to Confident Parenting

"But I don't want a shot!" my six year-old son wailed. We were in the doctor's office for a necessary immunization. But necessary or not, he certainly didn't want it! I hesitated and then said to our doctor, "I guess he doesn't want his shot today." We started to leave.

The doctor's reply startled me. "Since when do children decide these things? Who's the parent here?" I must have turned bright red with embarrassment. What was I thinking? Of course children don't like shots, but my son needed his and there was no reason to postpone it.

I turned to my son and said in the my best parental voice "Please get up on the table. You need to get your shot now. It will only hurt a little and be over very quickly." He did climb up on the table, got his shot with only a whimper and we were soon on our way home.

This little episode happened a dozen years ago but I still remember it vividly. What had come over me? Since when did I need someone to remind me that I, not my son, was "the parent"? Why did I need the doctor to embarrass me into acting like one?

I've been thinking about these questions since that day in the doctor's office, and I think I understand why so many other parents and I are often so hesitant. "When it comes to parenting, most of us already feel like it's being required to perform brain surgery in a dark room at midnight-blindfolded! We suspect there's a lot of critical information we don't know, and we don't even know what we don't know!"[1] Much of the time, parenting seems like a endless marathon. We all want desperately to "win" by raising successful children. But parenting is such a big responsibility!

For much of their early years, children seem so fragile and impressionable. Over and over, we hear how a child's fate in life depends almost entirely on the way the child is raised.[2] It's not just that our parenting is important, we're told it can be fatal if we handle our children wrong![3]

Most parents can identify with Frank's fears. He has a teenage daughter, and he's struggling with how strict to be in setting limits for her.

> If I get too hard, I'm afraid that she might turn and run. It's frustrating. I'm hoping and praying that she'll turn out all right. But there's no handbook, and I feel that if I haven't done any one thing just right, then I've failed."[4]

Desperately Looking For Help

Why all this fear of being a parent? In most societies and for most of history, parents just assumed they'd be successful. They took it for granted that their children would grow up to be normal, productive adults.[5] Whatever the challenges parents faced, they had a basic confidence that somehow they'd "get it right," at least most of the time.

That's no longer so with American parents today. We're afraid, hesitant, unsure of ourselves and unwilling to trust our own judgement. As Jack and Judith Baliswick observe in their excellent book *The Family: A Christian Perspective on the Contemporary Home,* instead of having confidence that our children will turn out alright in the end (as most children in most families have), we believe the opposite—that we'll fail as parents and ruin our children unless we have experts to feed us the formulas that guarantee success.[6]

So we've turned desperately to the experts for help; for some simple formula or technique that will enable us to parent without guilt and still be successful. After all, we are a technique-oriented society and there ought to be a technique for achieving success at anything-improving sales, better sex, even parenting.

All parents want to be successful in raising their children. But we've lost confidence in ourselves. We've become so unsure of our own parenting instincts that we plead, in effect, "Experts, please, tell us what to do!"

And they do! The sheer amount of books, magazines and other information offered to parents every day is overwhelming! Reading even most of it is virtually a full time job! One man complained that his wife "read everything that was ever published! She drove me crazy with Dr. Spock. There was a time when I could have punched him out!" Another woman said she "practically memorized dozens of child-rearing books and pamphlets."[7] Instead of the joyful, exhilarating time it should be, parenting must have seemed an anxious, fearful time for these folks. They were so frantically trying to discover the "secret" of successful parenting that they had no time to enjoy raising their children!

Experts All Around Us

Did you ever wonder how our parents made it without an expert to advise them on everything? When I was born, just after World War II, Dr. Spock's classic, *Baby and Child Care,*[8] had only just been published. My mother didn't have access to that book or a lot of others widely available to parents today.

There was one expert, however, who lived right in the same house: my grand-mother, her mother-in-law. She had given birth to 10 children, 6 of whom survived to become adults. So she had considerable experience and plenty of common sense wisdom to offer my mother.

And my mother needed all the help she could get. She had grown up in a privileged home near New York City. Her family wasn't rich, but it was very comfortable. Although her mother didn't work outside the home, they had a maid to do the cooking and cleaning. Though she was the oldest daughter, Mom didn't have to help care for her siblings. That was her mother's full time responsibility. So when she married my father and moved onto his farm in upstate New York, she really didn't know much at all about parenting.

If my grandmother's help wasn't enough for her, there was still more nearby. Just up the road in that little farming community lived a host of aunts and uncles, cousins and other relatives (including three of my father's siblings and their spouses). None of them had advanced degrees or publications to their credit, but they did have a wealth of experience and a lot of good, common sense. They provided a rich web of support and encouragement for each other's families throughout their active parenting years.

Too Important to Leave to Experts

Looking back, I can see some real advantages that our parents had in parenting us; advantages that we probably haven't had as we parent our own children. A generation or two ago, it was true that

By the time most people became parents, they had learned enough about child care to feel secure in raising their own children. When they did feel the need for advice, they could turn to their own parents and relatives....[9]

Much of this advice, of course, was based on the their experience and that of generations before them. It had stood the test of time and been proven in the lives of many, many families.

Today, parents face a world that is very, very different. The relatively simple world of a century ago has been replaced by a highly complex, fast changing, sometimes frightening world that seems to be careening out of control.

Our home today is in a typical suburban development. Everyone has their little "plot of earth" and works in a different place from the rest. I often describe our town to visitors as a group of housing developments around a shopping mall. There really isn't a town center or a "main street" gathering place. In fact, residents often decry the lack of community feeling there.

As adults and parents, our situation is not unlike that Rodney Clapp describes in his book, *Families at the Crossroads*:

> Here life is emphatically not of one piece. We work with one set of people and pray with another. We shop and play in an assortment of neighborhoods and communities. It is hard to know or be known. Friendship, so natural in the small town where we both grew up, must be pursued with intentionality and discipline. And even then, it may soon face the added challenge of distance: within the last five years, three of my closest friends have moved across the country.[10]

Many of us, like Rodney Clapp, don't have our parents or other relatives nearby to provide encouragement and support, either. They are "available to us only by phone or an occasional visit."[11]   And few of us have a live-in expert like my grandmother!

So what's a parent to do? The world may be different but we've still got to run the parenting race. Who's going to help us? Is there no alternative but to pore over book after book in a frantic search for the elusive secret to successful parenting? Is the secret to somehow discover the right "expert" and trust him or her with our children's future? I don't find those alternatives particularly appealing. There's an old saying that "politics is too important to leave to the politicians." The same can be said of parenting. It's just too important to leave to the "experts."

Can you imagine Aesop's fable of the Hare and the Tortoise including experts? If the Tortoise called in experts to ask their advice on how to win the race with the Hare, while they were talking, the hare could have woken up from his nap and still won the race twice! Besides, the tortoise already knew all that he needed to know; "Slow and Steady Wins the Race." If he was going to win, he knew he needed to get started, keep moving steadily ahead, and do his best! And it worked! In fact, that was the Tortoise's advantage. He may not have been the fastest, but he knew the challenge he faced, he knew what it took to win and he was determined to do his best. That's all he needed. He won the race.

You are the best parent your child can have. That's a foundational conviction of highly successful parents and the key to confident, successful parenting. Most of the time, you don't need to rely on experts. You **are** the expert! Be confident in your own ability and be determined to be the best parent you can be. You don't have all the answers (who does?), but you probably know more than you think. With confidence, determination, and God's grace, you can be a highly successful parent! You can win the race.

Recognizing Successful Parents

My wife and I have been parents for nearly 25 years. We have two sons. We've lived through all the anxieties, insecurities, and fears that most parents experience. We've battled the guilt, too. Along the way, we've learned some things I want to share with you through this book. Why? Because *I know that you can be a highly successful parent.* As we go through this book together, I'll share with you the convictions that guide successful parents and the qualities that characterize them. I'm convinced that you'll recognize that you already possess many of them, and that with prayer and effort, you can develop the rest!

As I've worked with parents over the years, I've observed that the highly successful ones are marked by certain characteristics. First, not being perfect, *successful parents are realistic.* They don't expect themselves or their children to be perfect, but they believe that by relying on common sense, good judgement, and hard work, they can be successful. "Successful" doesn't mean "perfect," however. They know that expecting perfection from any human being only leads to disappointment, failure, and guilt. This doesn't mean that successful parents set low standards for themselves and their children. On the contrary, they are committed to always doing their best as parents and they expect their children to do their best, also. In the end, highly successful parents believe that their best will be enough to make them highly successful.

I mentioned that successful parents rely on their common sense. Let me explain what I mean by "common sense." I can't define it any better than did Ray Guarendi and David Eich in their very helpful book, *Back To The Family.* Here's what they said: "Common sense means looking for the most simple, straightforward solution to solving a problem." It involves the "ability to make a reasonable decision based on what we know about a situation and what we want to achieve." In parenting,

25

common sense is deciding what to do based on your values, your family, and your children.[12]

So who is best qualified to make those decisions for your family? You are—not some anonymous "expert." **You** are the expert on your value system, your family and your kids. You know them better than anyone else. You are the person best qualified to make a reasonable decision and find simple, straightforward solutions to the parenting challenges you face. In most cases, all you need to do is use your common sense. That's not idealism or optimism. That's hard-headed realism.

Does that mean you should ignore all the advice that child development experts and others (even including me) offer you today? Not at all. Much of it can be very useful. *But whether and how it's useful is for you to decide.* Evaluate it on the basis of what you know about your particular family, the strengths and weaknesses of your family members, the wealth of knowledge you've gained from the daily experience of parenting, and your own common sense.[13] In the end, you are the best judge of what will work for your family. So take charge of your parenting. Trust your judgement.

Just one more word about "common sense." As you read further, you'll find occasional references to biblical passages and spiritual concerns. That's because I'm also convinced that the most realistic, highly successful parents follow the ancient, time tested wisdom found in the Bible. This gives them an extra dimension of good judgement—a "sanctified common sense" to guide them safely through the most challenging adventures of parenting.

With the help of sanctified common sense, all of us can be successful parents. By the time you've finished the following chapters, I trust you'll be convinced of that and well on your way to being the successful, confident parent you want to be.

Guilt-Free and Confident, Too!

Second, *highly successful parents are guilt-free parents.* Because they know they'll make mistakes now and then, they don't sit around blaming themselves and feeling like terrible failures as parents when their expectations are not always realized! While realistically acknowledging that they'll inevitably make an occasional mistake, they refuse to focus on faults, failures, and guilt (either theirs or their children's), and instead embrace a positive, guilt-free approach to parenting.

Third, *highly successful parents are confident parents.* They understand that, in almost any given instance, they (not some distant "expert") know what's best for their children. As a result, these parents expect to be successful. Each day won't be an unbroken string of successes, but over the long run, they're confident that they'll succeed as parents. And they expect their children will succeed, also.

Highly successful parents expect their child to be successful. That doesn't mean we become "little league fathers" or "stage mothers" who scream at our child if he or she isn't a star player on their team. It doesn't mean we become like the mother in Texas who was accused of trying to kill one of her daughter's classmates to ensure her daughter a place on the high school cheerleading squad. It doesn't mean we push our children to memorize the multiplication tables or learn to play the violin at the age of two. But it does mean that we let our child know that we always expect them to do their personal best. We assure them that real success is not measured in competition with others, but with themselves. True success is realized in terms of a child's own potential and her own goals and dreams.

Even when a child expects little of himself or sets goals unworthy of his potential, a successful parent "tries harder," knowing that children tend to live up (or down) to their parents' expectations. *Highly successful parents expect success from their children.* Sometimes, that's all it takes to begin to make their success real.

Of course, the temptation we parents face is measuring our own success by that of our children's. One pediatrician understands that temptation well. Parents assume, he says, that "if your kids aren't perfect, it must be your fault. That's a perfect case of setting yourself up for failure." Instead, he recommends that we "stop blaming ourselves every time something goes wrong."[14] We're not perfect and neither are our children.

There is real value in encouraging a child to strive for excellence and even to compete to be #1, whether in academics, athletics or any other pursuit. There are valuable lessons to be learned and benefits to be gained. But is being #1 the true measure of success for a child (or a parent)? If so, a lot of children-and parents-are doomed to be labeled as failures.

A better measure of successful parenting is given by the late Psychologist and child development expert, Dr. Bruno Bettleheim. He defines successful parenting as:

> ...the raising of a child who may not necessarily become a success in the eyes of the world, but who, on reflection, would be pleased with the way he was raised and who would decide that, by and large he is satisfied with himself, despite the shortcomings to which all of us are prey. I believe that another indication of having been raised well is a person's ability to cope reasonably well with the endless vicissitudes, the many hardships, and the serious difficulties he is likely to encounter in life and to do so mainly because he feels secure in himself.[15]

Bettleheim's words sound like common sense to me. Highly successful parents raise children who are happy with themselves. They are secure enough in their identities and values to be able to cope reasonably well with all the ups and downs of life and still find meaning and satisfaction from it. Add to that the crucial element of a strong and active faith, and you've got all the ingredients a child needs to grow up to be a happy, successful adult. In the end, isn't that the test of successful parenting? Isn't that what it means to win the parenthood "race"?

Believe in Yourself

We've seen that successful parents "try harder" to be the best parents they can be. Do they sometimes still make mistakes? Do they still have doubts about their decisions? Of course. But in spite of it all, they believe in themselves. They trust their judgement as parents. They believe that they know their child better than anyone else. And they believe that, in almost every case, they know what's best for their child better than anyone else, also-even (or perhaps, especially) an expert. Successful parents are confident in their own parenting.

Of course, there are some parents who admit they read through dozens of books and pamphlets on parenting when their first child was born. But other successful parents took a very different approach. "Initially," one mother said, "we read books by the experts. After our first child, we junked the books and relied on our intuition and backgrounds to raise our children."[16]

If you want to bake a cake, you can go to a cookbook. There you'll find the ingredients and the directions for baking a cake. Anyone who uses that cookbook and follows the directions should be able to produce the same kind of cake. That's what cookbooks are for. If you bake regularly, however, after a while you may stop using the cookbook. From experience or intuition (or both), you know what is needed without consulting a cookbook. Maybe you do use a "pinch" of this or a "dab" of that, but the cake still turns out just fine! You're an experienced, proven cake-baker, confident in your cooking skills. You don't need the cookbook anymore.

That's the kind of confidence highly successful parents develop, as they move steadily ahead and work hard to be the best parents possible to their children. As they go along in their parenting journey, these parents not only learn from their mistakes but they remember their successes, too! Their confidence grows and they begin to rely mostly on their own judgement and experience to guide them. They increasingly become their own experts.

When you think about it, trusting yourself really makes the most sense. After all, who is more of an expert on your family and your child than you? Who knows the situation you face and all the unique ingredients in your family as well as you? With the exception of the most severe and trying situations, most of us are our own best expert.

Of course, there is one significant problem with comparing children to cakes. If you use a cookbook carefully, you should be able to turn out cakes that are identical each time. Parenting is not so easy! Each child is unique—a special and precious individual created by God. No two can or should turn out alike.

Any parent who has more than one child knows this well. There are times when you might ask, "Is he really ours?" My two sons are both very special individuals; both are very precious to my wife and me. Still, their personalities are almost polar opposites.

Parenting is an adventure because children aren't like cakes that we can turn out uniform from a recipe. They aren't like computers that we can program for a guaranteed result. Computer users understand the truth of the maxim: "Garbage in, garbage out." If you feed misinformation into a computer, that's what you'll get back out. Thank God, that's not always the case with children. With resilience, they bear our mistakes, experiments, and failures and they continue to surprise and delight us.

So even though successful parents may read dozens of parenting books (such as this one!), they understand that these books are really "cookbooks." They're helpful, but only to a point. Since they know that there really isn't one set recipe for raising children, highly successful parents "pick and choose" the advice that fits their situation and their child's needs. The rest they leave—without worrying or feeling guilty. They are their family's own best expert and their child's best parent. They're confident in that.

We Try Harder

Fourth, *highly successful parents work harder at parenting.* They are not content to just "do enough" or "get by." They work harder than most other parents.

Do you remember the rental car company that always said it was #2 in the business? It then claimed "We Try Harder" because it wanted to be #1. "We Try Harder" could also be the slogan of highly successful parents. They know that parenting isn't easy so they try harder than most other parents in order to be successful. They're determined to do whatever it takes. Here's how one parent put it:

> To be a successful parent, we must be willing to do more than the average. We must be willing to supervise our children more closely, keep better contact with teachers, and work harder at discipline than do other parents. Excellent parenting means striving continually to improve, not to look better than others, but because that's the only kind of parenting we're content with.[17]

Trying harder means first of all being willing to put in the time it takes to be a highly successful parent—more time than many parents are willing to give. The Tortoise won the race not because he was fast, but because he was moving

CONFIDENT PARENTING IN CHALLENGING TIMES

while the Hare was sleeping! Children thrive on our time and attention just as plants thrive on sunshine. Successful parents work hard to give their children all the time and attention they need. And their hard work is key to their success.

Flexibility is Essential

Fifth, *successful parents are flexible parents.* That doesn't mean they can bend over backwards and touch the floor with their head, but it does mean bending and adapting their parenting practices to the growing and changing needs and capabilities of a child.

As our children grow older, they need our direct help and presence less and less, and our flexibility more and more. They need us to take our cues from them—stepping forward when they need us and stepping back when they don't.[18] A successful parent is "flexible enough to adapt to the growing capacities of the child, rather than remaining rigidly fixed in an outdated view of the child's abilities to manage things for himself."[19]

And this flexibility—like the physical kind—doesn't come easily. It takes discipline and practice. But without it we can get caught in the trap I've seen some parents fall into recently. One mother I know won't let her eight year-old daughter decide how much cereal to put in her bowl each morning. Though her daughter is quite capable of making that simple decision, her mother still controls it. It frustrates her daughter tremendously. "I'm not a four year-old anymore!" she cries. But her mother isn't flexible enough to recognize that and treat her accordingly.

There's also a thirteen year-old boy I know who faces a similar frustration. Fearful for his safety, his parents make him stay near the house to play when the other boys go to play at a neighbor's down the street. They're reluctant to let him go with his friends and their parents on weekend trips or retreats. They're over-protective of a boy his age. I see the frustration in his eyes as he wants to scream, "Why do you treat me like a little kid? I'm 13!" His parents aren't flexible enough to recognize that and treat him accordingly.

Flexibility is hard, but it's necessary. Flexing our parenting to match the changing needs of our children is one of the most difficult adjustments we must make. Yet, this flexibility is one of the marks of highly successful parenting.

Make a New Mistake

Sixth, *highly successful parents are always learning— from their mistakes and from other parents.* In fact, they gladly rely on other parents for advice and support whenever they need to.

I sang in a community choir for a number of years and learned some good lessons as well as a lot of good music. When we made mistakes, the director would go over the difficult part and help us learn it correctly. Then, he expected us to do it right the next time. He'd say, "You've learned that part now, so don't make that mistake again. Make a new mistake."

He didn't mind us making mistakes as long as we learned from them. In fact, he welcomed new mistakes as opportunities to learn. Most of all, he didn't want us to be afraid to try difficult passages just because we were afraid to make a mistake. Mistakes were no problem as long as we learned from past ones and went on to make new ones!

That's another attribute of parents who try harder. They're always learning from their mistakes. "The only way you can learn what to do right is by seeing what you do wrong."[20] After all, we tell our children to learn from their mistakes. So should we!

Successful parents know that they don't know it all. Much of their parenting skills come through on-the-job training, learning as they go. They know they'll make mistakes, but when they do, they accept their mistakes as educational opportunities, courses in the "College of Hard Knocks," and learn from them. Then, in challenging parenting times, they aren't afraid to trust their judgement, even if it means making a new mistake. Their motto would be "Good parents become better through mistakes."[21]

Highly successful parents are always willing to learn from other parents, also. They aren't reluctant to turn to other parents who have already gone or are going through the same stage of parenting that they are. These fellow parents can provide us with the support, encouragement and common sense that the extended family of grandparents, aunts and uncles once provided for our parents.

Support and encouragement are especially valuable when they come from other parents who share our faith and our goals for parenting. Don't neglect opportunities to take and to give that support in church classes and parenting groups. Share it informally during Bible studies or coffee hours. Successful parents are always learning—both from their mistakes and from other parents. That's one important reason they're successful!

In fact, research supports what common sense tells us: strong, healthy families are most often headed by parents who build friendships with other parents. When the going gets tough—as it surely does for all parents—these parents get going to seek out the help they need. They have a network of neighbors, friends, and fellow church members to provide help, advice and support.[22]

I've seen this network in action and maybe you have, too. When a baby is born prematurely and has to spend the first two months of life in the hospital, people bring the family meals, watch their children and keep vigil with the parents at the baby's bedside. They may not say a lot, but their presence speaks volumes.

When an eight year-old develops cancer, the entire church gathers to pray with the family and helps with transportation to treatment. They help provide a normal

34

schedule for the siblings while the parents are consumed with care for the sick one. By doing these things, a heavy burden is lifted from tired, weary backs.

A teenager becomes a substance abuser. Friends from the neighborhood and church gather in the home to affirm their love and respect for the parents. They pledge to help and they support treatment for the child. A smaller group meets weekly to encourage and assist the parents as they help their child through this difficult period. As a result, embarrassed and confused parents begin to regain hope that the family will recover. Life will be good again.

Even highly successful parents know they'll face problems. But they know they shouldn't—and needn't—face them alone. So, *they consciously build a network to turn to when help is needed.* This group of friends becomes an extended family of aunts and uncles and cousins and grandparents; "a group of people cheering (them) on and hoping for the best" for them.[23] This network is valuable insurance for getting through the tough times, and, as is the case with most insurance, it makes good sense to have it.

Single Parents Build Networks, Too

Single parents often find such a support network especially valuable. One single mother told how, after a particularly tough day, she was glad for good friends to turn to.

The day began when the police officer came to her door. Her daughter had pulled another girl's ponytail and kicked her book bag while they both were waiting for the school bus. The girl's mother charged harassment and called the police.

If that wasn't bad enough, before the day was over, another daughter announced she was in love with a gang member. The Police officer summed it up well: "It's tough being a single parent," he said.

It's no surprise she spent much of the day crying. She felt very much alone. But then, she remembered that she didn't have to be! "When single parenting gets tough, I've learned to rely on the people God has put in my life," she said. They provide the three essential things any single parent needs from time to time: companionship, comfort and care. She had good friends who would listen to her woes, who really cared about her and her children and would offer comfort and encouragement. They were her insurance to get her through those inevitable tough times.

Where does a single parent find a support system? If you're newly divorced, you may have lost many of the mutual friends and relatives who were once there for both you and your spouse. But most of us have some friends and relatives who've been around for a long time and stuck with us through the tough times. They're the ones who'll be the best support system, because it takes time to build strong, supportive relationships.

One insightful single mom, who had built a support network after her divorce, observed that vulnerability is important, also. Most people aren't mind readers. They're busy. They have problems. They don't automatically know that we need their help and support right now. So it's important to give them a call and let them know. "I really need to talk to someone for a few minutes. Is this a good time?" "I need to know someone is praying for me about this. Would you?" Vulnerability isn't easy, but as that single mom learned, it does build relationships that become the basis for your support system.[24]

Our Family's Network

When we moved away from our support network, our family learned how important it is to have one. During the fifteen years we lived in Pittsburgh, we lived in the same house and went to the same church. Over time, we built up a strong support base, made up primarily of fellow church members and some neighbors. We developed close friendships with other families who had started out with us as young couples and later became parents. They helped us through problems as small as coping with childhood illnesses and as large as facing the stresses of having a biracial foster child for five years.

Then, we moved to upstate New York, over 500 miles away. Suddenly, everything was new. We had no close friends nearby. We knew we could never replace the family of close relationships back in Pittsburgh, but that maybe we could build a new one in our new area. With a young teenager and one child in elementary school, we knew we had a lot of parenting challenges left to face! We needed an extended family of other parents with whom we could learn and share our experiences. As the months went on, we discovered that this group of people was already there and waiting for us in the new church family we joined.

That experience taught us a valuable lesson—that we need never be alone! No matter where we move, we have a family of brothers, sisters, aunts, and uncles and grandparents waiting to get to know us and support us—in our church, synagogue, or other shared interest group. Successful parents reach out to these people, learn from them, and also give to them. That's what helps make them successful!

The Expert of Experts

Finally, *highly successful parents rely on God as the most trusted expert of all.* In his book, *Back to the Family,* Dr. Ray Guarendi says, "God is the ultimate childrearing expert, the One sought, not just during trying times, but daily."[25] This is the one expert that all successful parents happily rely on. He is the ultimate source of their good judgement and common sense and the only completely reliable source of their confidence as parents.

Dr. Guarendi quotes an old parenting maxim: "From birth to six, you teach them; from six to twelve, you guide them; and from twelve to eighteen, you pray for them."[26] He says that good parents bend that formula a little because they know that praying for their child begins at birth (even if it does tend to reach a peak during the teen years!).

And highly successful parents turn to this "expert of experts" in prayer daily! They know that God alone is the one expert who not only understands their children even better than they do, but also loves their children even more than they do! They know this parent is one expert whose judgement they can always trust. When trusting God, they find their parenting judgement deepened and strengthened. That trust also gives them the confidence they need to meet even the greatest parenting challenges successfully.

Highly successful parents recognize that there's nothing we parents face that God doesn't understand. The parenting principles and guidelines set out in the Bible are, in a real sense, a user's manual of proven principles and guidelines for us to rely on in raising our children. These principles and guidelines help us understand how our children function and how to give them what they need in order to grow up as healthy, happy, productive adults. After all, God, our heavenly parent, is the parent of our children along with us. He is the most reliable expert to which we earthly parents can turn.

Restoring the Proper Balance

It was less than thirty years ago that the late Dr. Benjamin Spock gave this advice to parents: "Don't take too seriously all that the neighbors say. Don't be overawed by what experts say. Don't be afraid to trust your common sense. Bringing up a child won't be a complicated job if you take it easy, trust your own instincts, and follow the directions your doctor gives you."[27] Dr. Spock's approach in his books was to give parents general information about child development and general guidelines to follow in applying it. Then, as the quote above illustrates, he (and others like him) expressed the trust that, as parents observed their child in the course of daily care, they would use their common sense and good judgement to be successful parents.

When he wrote that advice in 1968, however, the notion that successful parenting was largely a matter of common sense and good judgement was already being replaced by the perception that parents could not succeed without knowledge of the proper parenting "techniques." Experts told parents they needed to understand as much about child development and psychology as possible so they could apply specific scientific techniques and rules to each of the many and varied parenting situations they encountered. If they didn't, it was implied, they risked permanent harm to their children and certain failure as parents.[28] No wonder parents began to feel overwhelmed, hesitant and inadequate!

As we've noted, highly successful parents are confident parents. They recognize that they don't know it all, but they believe that they do know enough and have enough good judgement to be what the late Dr. Bruno Bettleheim called successful, "good enough parents."[29]

As I've observed parents over twenty-five years of training and encouraging them, this has become clear to me: *Most parents are, by far, the real "experts" at parenting their children. On the whole, they know far better than anyone else what is best and works best for their children. Using their "sanctified common sense" (common sense bolstered by prayer) and good judgement, they have all they need to be confident, successful parents.*

I can imagine that the anxiety and sense of inadequacy that most parents feel today is magnified in single parents who don't have a trusted spouse with whom to check their instincts. I've never been a single parent but

I've known many very successful ones. So I know that the basic principles I've set out here also apply to single parents. *Single parents, too, are their family's own best "expert." They too can trust their judgement in meeting the parenting challenges they face. They too can be confident, successful parents.*

So, while there are no easy answers to successful parenting, with common sense, hard work and determination, you can succeed. Not only **can** you succeed, you will! When you finish this book, I trust you'll feel a renewed sense of confidence in your ability to be a successful parent. Then, if you say to yourself, "I guess I'm a pretty good parent after all," I'll be very pleased. Most importantly so will you—and your children!

Chapter 2

Relax! Nobody's Perfect!

It was a startling public confession. "I'm the worst mother in the world!" she said tearfully. This was not some child—abuser breaking down in court, however. Those words were spoken by popular television talk show host Kathie Lee Gifford during her program one morning. What had prompted her to make such a harsh self-evaluation? When he was four and a half months old, her son, Cody, strapped in a car seat and sitting on the kitchen counter, had reached for a toy and fallen over. He wasn't badly hurt, but Kathie Lee's self-image as a mother certainly was.[1]

A painful fact of life that all parents discover early in their parenting journey is that nobody's perfect. Parents are, after all, people first. And just as there are no perfect people, there are no perfect parents. There never were and never will be! We all begin our parenting with high hopes that we'll be the wisest, most loving, and responsible (practically perfect) parents in history. The problem is that parenting is much more an art than a science. As one wise pediatrician observed, we soon discover that "raising children is on the job training. You figure out by trial and error what works and what doesn't."[2]

Anyone who's been a parent very long recognizes the truth in that. Parenting brings plenty of trials and lots of errors! In fact, "very good parents who raise very good children are going to make half a dozen child rearing mistakes a day."[3] As a result, one parent observed, "scratch most parents and we bleed guilt!"[4]

In an earlier book, *It's The Little Things That Count,*[5] I wrote of some of the rituals and traditions that our family has observed over the years: camping trips, family vacations and other "little things" that make up who we are as a family. When my college student son gave the book to some of his friends, they teased him about belonging to the "Beaver" family (I suppose they really meant the Cleavers of "Leave It To Beaver" fame). Boy, did we have them fooled! As much as I was pleased by the compliment, I knew it wasn't true. Families are made up of people and since there are no perfect people, there are no perfect families, either; certainly not mine!

In fact, expecting that we'll be perfect parents who raise perfect children is a myth, and a very dangerous one.[6] It sets us up for failure, disappointment and discouragement. Common sense tell us that "mistakes are as much a part of parenting as kids are."[7] That may sound like bad news, but highly successful parents don't see it that way! *They're realistic about human nature. They know they'll make mistakes*—every parent does! And they know that feeling guilty and depressed about an occasional parenting failure doesn't do anyone any good!

But successful parents know that there's good news, too! Even though we can't be perfect parents, it doesn't matter! God, in his wisdom, arranged it so that we don't need to be perfect! He made human (imperfect) children to be raised by human (imperfect) parents. And despite imperfect parenting, most children turn out just fine!

Every child in history has been raised by imperfect parents just like us. That's the only kind of parents there are! So even if we aren't perfect parents, we can still be highly successful. As long as you are the best parent you can be, you can relax. Give yourself a break![8] In fact,

Honest mistakes made by loving parents do not damage children psychologically, not now or at some unknown juncture down the road. They only make life a little tougher for awhile, for all involved, but they don't ruin "psyches." Kids are built to withstand being raised by human beings, with all our shortcomings and inconsistencies. They are remarkably resilient, some capable not only of surviving the most emotionally turbulent environments, but maturing against all odds into well adjusted adults.[9]

Our children don't need perfect parents, but they do need loving ones.[10] *We all make mistakes, but nurtured by our love, our children survive and thrive!*

Children Grow Up To Be....

Did you ever have the experience of really "blowing it" in front of your children? Maybe you disciplined them unfairly or they heard you call someone an unkind name. Since your children clearly saw you make a mistake, there was only one thing you could do—admit it and apologize. If you've done that, my guess is that almost every time, your children were eager to forgive you. They were probably easier on you than you were on yourself. Why is that? Because they already know they aren't perfect, and it's a great relief for them to see that you aren't either! If you aren't perfect, then they know they don't have to be!

That's really good news to children. It's hard to be happy when they're carrying around the heavy burden of the need to be perfect. They believe their parents expect it of them and perhaps, that their parents' love for them is conditioned on it. Then the problem becomes that, since they know they can't be perfect, they also can't be sure that they're loved!

I have a little plaque in my study that I bought at a bookstore some years ago. It expresses a simple, yet profound parenting truth: *"Children Grow Up To Be the Love They've Known."* I keep it where I can see it every day to remind me that the love my children receive in our home will shape their hearts and lives daily as they grow and make their way in the world. Every time I read it, I'm reminded to ask, "Just what kind of love are my children receiving in our family?" Is it unconditional, "no matter what" love that accepts and affirms them, imperfections and all? Or is it a harsh, critical, "love" that holds them to a standard of perfection that even I can't attain? I'm so grateful that others are patient with my failings. Though I'm in mid-life, "God isn't finished with me yet." With my children, he's only begun!

Children are like an unfinished string quartet or painting. They're "works in progress." There are still many beautiful chords to be written, many skillful brushstrokes to be added. Only then, will the full beauty of God's work in their lives be clear. As they grow, the quibbles and quarrels, tempers and teasing remain. *"Children Grow Up To Be the Love They've Known."* I need to love them with a kind and patient love as their heavenly father does. He's doing wonderful work in them, but he's not finished yet.

The kind of love my children (and my spouse) need from me has best been described this way: "Love is patient, love is kind...it is not self-seeking, it is not easily angered, it keeps no record of wrongs."[11] They need this love even if it is the third time today that child tracked mud on the living room carpet! It's love that "forgives and forgets." When love forgives a wrong, it promptly forgets it! Then, it looks forward to a "right" in the future.[12] That's just the kind of love that imperfect people—especially children—really need.

Hummingbird or Vulture?

Hummingbirds and vultures are very different kinds of birds in many ways, but both live in the desert. As the vulture flies over the sand, it looks anxiously for signs of death. It feeds on death—on the rotting victims of that harsh environment. A hummingbird, by contrast, flies over the same wasteland with a very different goal. It looks for signs of life. It trains its eye to sight the beautiful, blooming desert plants from which it will draw sweet food. It's ironic that while the hummingbird and the vulture live in the same environment, one feeds off life, and the other, death. Can it be that, as they fly over the same harsh desert, each finds only what it is looking for?

We parents often function the same way as these birds of the desert. We tend to notice in our children mostly what we are looking for. If we see our children (or spouse) with eyes looking for imperfections, that's exactly what we'll find! It's hard to really love a child when that's all you see, isn't it? And it's harder for a child to feel loved when she's always seen through vulture eyes, and always feels criticized and rotten. But parents deal in life, not death! Highly successful parents look at their children with hummingbird eyes. Seeing the beauty of their blossoming personalities puts them in a much more positive light! Seeing them as "works of God in progress," gives us a whole new perspective on them.

Perhaps you have a strong willed child in your family. You could think of her as stubborn, with all the negative connotations that label carries. On the other hand, you could just as easily see her as tenacious, a valuable, positive personality trait. That's the difference between the perspective of a hummingbird and that of a vulture! While we may not be able to overlook our child's flaws, such a simple change in perspective allows us to look past those flaws to discover the growing beauty of God's work within them. That's what our children need from us! We need to be more like hummingbirds, not vultures!

Dirt or Diamonds?

I grew up on a dairy farm in upstate New York. My father grew corn and oats each year to feed the cows over the winter. As a boy, I can remember watching him plow the fields every spring before planting. The soil was quite fertile and, in its own way, quite beautiful. But as the spring rains fell, that rich, beautiful soil turned to messy, brown mud. When that mud made its way onto my boots and into the house (as it inevitably did), it suddenly lost its beauty and became just plain old unwelcome dirt!

Farmers aren't the only ones who deal with dirt. In a very real sense, every family does. Quarreling children, a teen whose room looks (and smells) like a landfill, and other everyday conflicts, tensions, failures, and frustrations are at least as unsettling and unwelcome as dirt tracked onto a freshly clean floor. And in families made up of imperfect people, they're just as inevitable, too! But miners also deal with dirt for a living. They don't plow and cultivate it, of course. They dig and sift it. What's the point of their labor? They're looking for precious minerals. Surrounded by the dirt and hidden in it are jewels, gold and silver.[13]

Although both mineral miners and farmers work in the dirt, miners have a very different perspective. The miner sees the dirt and has to deal with it, but it's not the focus of his attention or efforts at all. His eyes are trained to look **through** the dirt to find the tiny, precious diamonds and minerals hidden in it. For the miner, a load of dirt is a treasure chest! That's a pretty useful perspective for imperfect parents living in imperfect families, isn't it? Each day brings a load of "dirt" we've got to deal with, but it needn't divert our attention from the real pleasures and

46

rewards of family life: uncovering and celebrating the precious "diamonds" in those we love.

Do you remember the early days of your courtship and marriage? I wrote little poems to my wife and even tried writing a song or two (which, mercifully, haven't survived!). I just knew she was perfect, and I was totally enthralled with her perfection. In those early days of romance, the stars in our eyes allow us to see only such an idealized image of our beloved. But after a few months of marriage, reality begins to set in. All of a sudden, our spouse doesn't look so perfect anymore. We discover that he is sloppy around the house or careless with the family finances (both are some of my vices!). She can't cook, doesn't like football, and has political opinions that you find strange at best. Is your marriage on the rocks?

This is when it's important to practice diamond mining. In addition to his failures, perhaps your husband is also a conscientious spouse who'll make a great father. Perhaps cooking isn't her strength, but she is a good companion and will make a great mother. When the imperfections of our spouse or children are all we see, we forget that nobody's perfect. We begin to assume the worst about those we love the best. A harsh, critical spirit infects our family relationships. Then, we are really in trouble!

Highly successful parents (and spouses, too) focus on the diamonds, not the dirt in family life. Your children and your spouse may be diamonds in the rough, but they're precious diamonds, nonetheless. You'll deal with plenty of dirt in daily family life, so keep it in perspective. Over years of (sometimes painful) experience, our family has applied a little rule that helps us keep things in perspective during the difficult times of family life. We call it The DSSS Rule: "Don't Sweat the Small Stuff."

When, as children, we complained of some terrible injustice done to us by a sibling, my mother would often say "Don't make a federal offence out of everything." That was her way of saying "Relax. Don't Sweat The Small Stuff. Nobody's perfect."

A lot of the problems of family life are really just "small stuff." Highly successful parents are not always able to excuse things, but sometimes, in love, they won't "sweat" them, either. They keep things in perspective. They use the eyes of a hummingbird. They look for diamonds in the dirt. They *follow the DSSS Rule: Don't Sweat The Small Stuff!*

Learn From Your Mistakes

More than one mother has uttered Kathie Lee Gifford's cry, "I'm the worst mother in the world!" and really meant it. We aren't perfect. We will make mistakes. Mistakes by parents are as inevitable as dirty diapers and spilt milk. And that's not all bad, either. After all, mistakes are not so much examples of our failures as examples of our love.[14] We can learn from them, build on them, and move on toward our goal of being the best parents we can be.

However, for some people, building from our mistakes is easier than for others. We've come to adulthood haunted by painful memories of our own parents' mistakes. We were abused or neglected. Perhaps we were hurried through childhood and resent never having had one. It's easy to repeat those mistakes with our own children.

One woman, the eldest of five children, recalls how her mother always seemed overwhelmed by the responsibilities of raising them. So from the time she was twelve years-old, she was expected to be the "assistant mother." She did much of the cooking and cleaning and helped care for her younger siblings. To this day, she speaks of her childhood with some pain. For her, being the best parent she can be has meant letting go of resentment and regret so she can let her own children enjoy being children!

For the 150 million adults in the U.S. today who grew up in dysfunctional families, being a successful parent is even more difficult.[15] They're adult children of alcoholics, survivors of incest, children of divorce and countless others. They've had to struggle hard to avoid making similar mistakes in their own parenting. I've read their stories and seen the positive results of their efforts with my own eyes.[16] You probably have, too. With "reverse resolve," they've determined to rise above their negative upbringing and reverse the harmful personality traits and parenting patterns they've carried from childhood.[17] They've learned from their parents' mistakes, built something good on them and then moved on to become highly successful parents. They give hope to all of us. Maybe you're one of them!

Buy The Best and Junk The Rest

When I was a boy, the local used car dealer in our area advertised with the slogan "We Buy the Best and Junk the Rest." That was his way of saying he could recognize quality when he saw it, benefit from it, and not waste his energies on anything else. He built a successful used car business on that simple slogan. That's a good piece of advice for parents, too. *Learn to recognize good parenting when you see it in yourself and in others. Benefit from it, and put aside the rest.*

Of course, the way that most of us learn parenting is from our own parents. We model after the parenting we've received. But what if your own parents weren't good models and, as a result, you're not confident in your own parenting? Then look around you. Neighbors, friends, and fellow church members may offer some models of very good persons who are also good parents. Learn from them and build on their examples and advice. Learn from their mistakes too, as well as your own. Take the best and junk the rest. Then, move ahead toward your goal of becoming a successful parent.

Our family had a foster daughter some years ago. She had been abandoned by her mother at eighteen months. When Antoinette came to us, she was four years old and had already lived in two other foster homes. At that time, my oldest son was just five and my youngest hadn't been born yet. Over the next five years, my relatively new and still developing parenting skills and instincts were sorely tried.

I thought I understood the value of structure and consistency in providing security for this little girl who'd seen so little of it during her short life. But it seemed that the more structure (rules) I provided and the more consistent I was, the more we ended up in fights and power struggles. I knew how to "win," but the struggles grew worse and worse. As the months went on, Antoinette got more and more angry and I got more and more frustrated. When the courts returned her to her mother five years later, I admit that my sadness was mixed with relief! I came to the painful conclusion that, at least in foster parenting, I was a failure.

In the decade since then, I've had a lot of time to reflect on my mistakes. I've had some good opportunities to discuss that situation with other parents. As a result, I've learned a lot about my approach to parenting and about myself. If I could do this foster parenting over again, I know I'd do much better. This time I'd understand that this little girl felt powerless and helpless so much of the time. I'd understand that so many of our struggles were her way of telling me she needed to feel a little power of her own. I'd have given her more choices. I'd have known when to be flexible. I'd have.... Well, I still wouldn't be perfect, but I'd sure be different!

Believe me, I've wrestled with a lot of guilt over that experience. I learned a lot about myself and my weaknesses as a parent. I can be stubborn. I can be selfish. I'm nowhere near being a perfect parent. I've felt guilty. Maybe you have, too. That guilt confronts us with two simple choices: either forgive ourselves, learn from our mistakes, and move on, or be paralyzed and ineffective as a parent.

Guilt can make us so unsure of ourselves and so afraid to be wrong that we're afraid to really trust ourselves to ever be good parents again.

Here's where successful parents learn to forgive and forget. God, in his love, forgives us. So we can forgive ourselves. It's as if God puts all our failures as parents in a big lake. Then, he builds a barbed wire fence around the lake and puts up a sign that says "Keep Out! No Fishing!" He forgives and forgets. Every day is a fresh start. So we can forgive ourselves and accept each new day with its parenting challenges as a gift from God.

And in addition to forgiving ourselves, we must forget our failures, also. Highly successful parents recognize the ancient advice that is still sound today; "Forgetting what is behind and straining toward what is ahead, I press on toward the goal."[18] We may not be able to literally forget our past failures, but we can put them behind us, refuse to dwell on them and decide to work at being better parents.

That's been my goal. Today, I'm still not a perfect parent, but I am a wiser and better one. I've learned from my failures in the past and resolved to do better in the future. If you've been paralyzed by guilt from past parenting failures, I invite you to join me in forgetting what is behind and straining toward what is ahead—being a confident, highly successful parent.

Children Learn From Our Mistakes

Of course, some parenting challenges are simply beyond our control. Sometimes we do our best and nothing works. We often blame ourselves for our children's behavior, even though we can't always prevent it. Our children ultimately make their own choices. And they're not perfect either. We shouldn't always feel guilty.

But whether parenting problems come as a result of our failures or not, the result is the same—pain. In our pain, we realize that there really is only one thing to do; lean on the "heavenly parent," the one who loves our children even more than we do. Pain slows us down. It quiets us by its sheer weight. In our pain, we grow quiet enough to recognize God is at work in it. He is walking through our pain with us. God is the only hope we have of getting through what often seems unbearable. In fact, God works through our pain and helps us continue growing toward being better and better parents.[19] He's not made any mistakes, but he has had plenty of pain as a parent. God understands. God can help.

Our mistakes have one other surprising benefit. They provide a great opportunity to show our children how to learn from them. You can show them how you handle failure, learn from it and move ahead. That's an invaluable life lesson! Many parents think they should hide their mistakes and weaknesses from their children. "On the contrary," says Seattle Pediatrician Robert Hauck. "It's positive for children to see you fail. If children think their parents are perfect, they have a model they can never copy. It's your duty to show your children you are fallible-that you get angry, procrastinate and make poor judgement calls. Teach your children that they will grow up and be imperfect just like you, and that's OK."[20]

As we have seen, our children often secretly fear that their parents are perfect (at least until they get to be teenagers and then they know better!). Children know they never can be, but wanting to please, they try and try, and fail and fail! Or they decide not to try so that they're not disappointed by their inevitable failure! What a position for a child to be in! Admitting our mistakes teaches our children to accept themselves and others who, like them, fail from time to time. It also models how to handle mistakes before God—that the one who makes a mistake admits it, is forgiven and affirmed, and moves on to learn and do better the next time.

That car dealer's slogan is a good rule for all parents to follow. Buy the best—learn from your mistakes. Junk the rest—put your mistakes behind you. Accept God's forgiveness and continue on your parenting journey!

It's Still a Mystery

Encouragement for imperfect parents sometimes comes from the strangest places! On one episode of his popular television series, *The Cosby Show*, Bill Cosby, as Cliff Huxtable, was congratulated by one of his daughters on being such a great parent. He replied wisely, "There are no great parents, only great children." I think what Cosby meant was that, in the end, the secret to good parenting is still shrouded in mystery. We never know how our efforts will turn out until our children do. And each turns out unique.

> "Each child loves particular games and certain sorts of songs, has a taste for broccoli or cauliflower, is frightened by this animal or that-all according to an intricate weave, here of mother's traits, here of father's attitudes, here of both parents' habits and finally of the child's own incomprehensible and original predilections."[21]

So however they turn out, we're only partially responsible. We can't take all the credit, and we don't deserve all the blame. There's so much unknown, so much we can't control and, of course, so many choices that only they can make. When our children turn out great (as most of them do), it's just another mystery of the grace of God. We had imperfect childhoods. Our own parents, our first models for parenting, were, like us, imperfect. We make a half-dozen mistakes a day, and yet our children continue to love us and forgive us—again and again and again.

Sandra Wilson, in her very helpful book, *Shame Free Parenting*, tells of her choice for her favorite Bible verse. She admits that most people would find it a strange one.[22] It's from the book of Jonah, chapter three, verse one; "Then, the Word of the Lord came to Jonah a second time."[23]

Jonah was a rebellious and reluctant prophet. He received an assignment from God to take a message to the wicked city of Ninevah and command them to repent of their rebelliousness. If they did, God could forgive them and not punish them. But, even though God's patience and love were evident to him, Jonah boldly said "No!" He didn't want to obey. That's when God saw to it that Jonah had some time to reconsider his decision. He gave Jonah a three day "vacation," free of distractions, in the belly of a great fish. There was no television to watch or no video games to play—nothing to do but think. After this timeout, Jonah decided to accept his assignment. God gave Jonah a second chance to get it right.

"Then, the word of the Lord came to Jonah a second time" is a verse every parent should memorize! Perfect people don't need second chances, but God, in his grace, knows that parents often do. So over and over again he provides what we need—second, third, fourth chances, and more! Every day is a "fresh start day" made possible by God's grace. And, every day, our children are channels of God's grace to us. They are wonderfully resilient in the face of our mistakes. The great mystery of it all is that they usually turn out superbly!

"Nobody's perfect," either as a person or a parent, but somehow, it doesn't matter! After all, our children don't need perfect parents, they just need loving ones. A teacher at an Ivy League school once compared good teaching to good parenting. You can see that he could have been talking about highly successful parenting, too!

Like mothering or parenting, good teaching is not a matter of specific techniques or styles, plans or actions. Like friendship, good teaching is not something that can be entirely scripted, pre-planned or pre-specified. If a person is thoughtful, caring and committed, mistakes will be made but they will not be disastrous; if a person lacks commitment, compassion, or thought, outstanding technique and style will never really compensate. Teaching is primarily a matter of love. The rest is, at best, ornamentation, nice to look at but not of the essence; at worst it is obfuscating-it pulls our attention in the wrong direction and turns us away from the heart of the matter."[24]

Putting it another way, if you want to be a highly successful parent, it's more important to have the heart of a parent than a complete and comprehensive understanding of childrearing mechanics. The kind of person you are will have far more impact on your children than whether or not you can reflect feelings with the precision of a counselor or whether your discipline is always consistent.[25] Our children are shaped by the kind of people we are. They carry within them something of the heart we carry within us.

The key to successful parenting is to recognize where good parenting begins; in good "personing." What matters is not that we are perfect but what kind of person we are. "Our personhood sets the tone for our parenthood."[26] Highly successful parents are convinced that *if you want to be a better parent, you must work at being a better person.* So take a serious look at yourself once in a while. Ask others whom you trust what kind of person you are, where you are strong and where you can do better. What is your faith like? Is it growing? Focus on improving some areas (begin with just one or two) that will make you a better person. You still won't be a perfect parent, but you will be a much better one.

And if disappointment with your imperfect parenting ever threatens to overwhelm you, take comfort in this little jingle:

The definition of perfect parenting
is easy to express.
Just err and err and err again,
but less and less and less.[27]

That's a goal you can reach! Just remember how highly
successful parents do it. Rely on God. Love your children.
Be the best person you can be. Forgive and Forget. Then,
relax! After all, nobody's perfect!

Chapter 3

How Healthy is Your Tree?

Whenever a new baby comes home from the hospital, grand-parents, aunts and uncles, and other relatives begin to play an old but fascinating game. As they sit in the living room admiring the new baby, visiting friends and neighbors play it, too. When the baby goes out in public, even strangers play it.

The games is called "who does the baby look like?" "He's got his dad's hands." "She's got her mom's eyes." It's a game based on a common sense notion that no one questions: A baby ought to resemble its parents.

We enjoyed playing that game when our boys were born. In fact, we enjoyed it so much we still play a version of it today. When people visit our home for the first time, we often point to pictures of our two sons displayed prominently. The pictures were taken when each was exactly the same age and they're wearing similar outfits. It's fun to ask friends to guess which son is which and which of their parents they most resemble.

The sharing of physical characteristics is the earliest and most obvious mark of parental influence on children. But as babies grow up, their family resemblance begins to take on more than just physical characteristics. They also begin to share their parent's attitudes, habits, and moral and spiritual values.

Dr. Penelope Leach observes, "It's as if children are apprenticed to parents in the business of growing up. They learn by watching, talking and sharing with them. They develop their values from the way you behave as a person (with everybody, not just with them) and they base their behavior even more on what you **do** than what you say."[1]

Most of the time, parents are reasonably happy with what they see of their lives and values reflected in their children. But others, like the father in Harry Chapin's song "Cat's in the Cradle," feel very differently. Having realized that there were some real deficiencies in his own life, he regretted that his son had "grown up just like me. My boy was just like me."[2]

It should be no surprise. "The acorn doesn't fall far from the tree" has long been a common sense way of recognizing that *parents are not only the first, but usually the most powerful role models for their children.* Highly successful parents are convinced of that and that conviction shapes and influences all their parenting.

Who's Your Child's Hero?

A few years ago, Dade County, Florida (which includes the city of Miami) instituted a curfew for children under 17 years of age. With a few careful exceptions, young people there now have to be home by 11 p.m. on week nights and midnight on weekends.[3]

And that action was not an isolated one. As Dade County was effecting a curfew, the mayor of Schenectady, NY, near where I live, proposed a similar one. Other municipalities around the country are also expected to begin acting "in loco parentis," a phrase that means "in the place of parents."

58

Where have all the parents gone so that governments need to act in their places? They're stressed out by demanding jobs and over-loaded schedules. With both parents working in many families, neither Mom nor Dad has either the time or energy to teach their children responsible, mature behavior; from manners, to respect for other's property, to when to go to bed, to moral and spiritual values.

Children in single parent families may suffer even more, despite the heroic efforts of many single parents. Most single parents are mothers overburdened by carrying the entire responsibility for their children's financial and parenting needs. With some wonderful exceptions, the fathers are often uninvolved. The National Commission on America's Urban Families concluded that "the single greatest factor contributing to our most serious social ills is the erosion of the two parent home."[4]

With fewer parents willing and able to be role models and teachers for their children, governments, like Dade County and Schenectady, try desperately to fill the gap. It's true that "government doesn't raise children, parents do." But why **can't** government raise children, especially if parents don't? The answer lies in the fact that government can't provide what children need most in order to grow into responsible, self-disciplined, faith-filled adults: committed, consistent role models and authority figures who, out of an unconditional love for them, will invest the tremendous time and energy needed to guide their lives into mature adulthood. Only parents can do that. Who else would?

Good Parenting Begins With...

And children don't just need their parents to be their models, they want them to be. Does that surprise you? A survey of 21,000 nine and ten year-old children asked them who was their greatest hero. The children overwhelmingly named their parents. It's hard to disagree with the survey's conclusion (although I have a feeling the answer might have been radically different if they'd asked teenagers!) "Children are looking for role models and they are looking close to home....It seems to me that our children are telling us loud and clear: Please act like the role models we want you to be."[5]

Highly successful parents are convinced that they must be intentional, positive role models for their children. That means demonstrating, as well as discussing, over and over, as consistently as you can, the moral and spiritual values and attitudes that make for a responsible, self-disciplined adult. Does that mean you have to be perfect? Of course not. As we saw in chapter 2, perfection is neither possible nor necessary. But as role models for their children, successful parents are doing the best job they can to be the kind of people they want their children to become. In other words, what matters is not that we are perfect but what kind of person we are. "Our personhood sets the tone for our parenthood."[6]

Here's how one mother, nationally known writer Anna Quindlen, puts it:

> A child doesn't merely grow up to be good, in the way she will be blond or bow-legged; if she's to develop a moral intelligence, as Pulitzer prize winner Robert Coles has termed it, it will take a considerable effort on the part of her parents. We must not only be good parents, but good people.[7]

In short, highly successful parents live by the conviction that *Good Parenting begins with Good Personing*. If you want to be a better parent and the hero your child wants and needs, first commit to being a better person.

For some of us, that means taking a good, hard look at ourselves. I'm sure you want your children to be honest. Do you report every dollar of income on your tax returns? Do you refuse to let your small 12 years old pay the "under

12" admission price? Do you tell your children to tell unwelcome telephone callers that you're not home when you clearly are? Do you make attending public worship a top priority in your life, even when you're tired or on vacation? You aren't perfect, but are you setting a consistent, positive example? Are you growing as a person—and as a person of faith?

Highly successful parents don't get bogged down trying to master parenting techniques or formulas from experts. They know that having the heart of a parent is more vital to successful parenting than understanding childrearing techniques. The kind of person you are will impact your children far more than any techniques or parenting "formulas."

It's encouraging to realize "the great impact of modeling on a child's learning. It means that parents do not have to be brilliant analysts of their children's psyches; they need not possess commanding overviews of educational theory" but they do need to "lead the kind of lives they hope their children will lead [and] be the kind of people they hope their children will be."[8] "The acorn doesn't fall far from the tree." And highly successful parents are regularly asking themselves "How healthy is my tree?"

It's no surprise that emotionally and spiritually healthy parents tend to raise emotionally and spiritually healthy children. Compassionate parents tend to raise compassionate children. Parents with a deep faith commitment tend to pass that on to their children. Our children grow up to be like us; shaped by the kind of people we are and carrying within them many of the same passions that we carry within us.

This is expressed so well in these familiar words of Dorothy Law Nolte:

> If children live with criticism,
>   they learn to condemn.
> If children live with hostility,

61

they learn to fight.
If children live with ridicule,
 they learn to be shy.
If children live with shame,
 they learn to feel guilty.
If children live with tolerance,
 they learn to be patient.
If children live with encouragement,
 they learn confidence.
If children live with praise,
 they learn appreciation.
If children live with fairness,
 they learn justice.
If children live with security,
 they learn to have faith.
If children live with approval,
 they learn to like themselves.
If children live with acceptance and friendship,
 they learn to find love in the world.[9]

Raising "Good" Children

What kind of children do you want to raise? Like most of us, you probably want your children to grow up to be people who care about others, have a sensible attitude toward material things, and possess a strong and clear set of moral and spiritual values.

How do you raise a child that is caring and compassionate? If you are, or are trying to become, such a person yourself, it will be natural for you to talk about the feelings and cares of others with your children. When our boys were very young, my wife would talk with them about how their favorite teddy bear "felt" if he was handled roughly or left behind when they went out to play. As they got older, she would continue to talk with them about the feelings and concerns of their playmates and friends. When a friend was mean to them ("I guess he doesn't feel very good about himself today") or they were inadvertently insensitive to others ("Won't he be hurt if you don't include him, too?"), she'd help them share the feelings of others and encourage them to do the caring thing. I'm sure that's a big part of the reason they are such caring young men today.

Children aren't born with sensitivity and empathy for others. They are basically egocentric and largely unable to consider the feelings of others until they reach the age of three or four. As every parent knows, even older children can be incredibly insensitive and self-centered. Their capacity for empathy and compassion must be carefully nurtured by our words and example—literally from birth. That way, as opportunities to show caring for others arise, they'll know how to do it!

Many parents want to teach their children compassion for the poor. But if your family, like ours, lives in a fairly affluent community, that's not easy. It's hard for a young child to care about people they've never seen!

One small way to teach your children care for the poor is to take them to help at the local city mission or your church's food pantry. Make it a regular practice so your children are able to get to know some of the folks they serve and learn that caring isn't just a one-time event. Help your children provide a gift at Christmas for needy children in the community (your church probably knows some).

My wife is a teacher in an inner city school. Many of the children she teaches lack things our children take for granted. One Christmas, she proposed that we forego a portion of what we spend on presents in order to buy a gift certificate to the local grocery store for a needy family whose child was in her class. It was a small thing, admittedly, but one concrete way our family could demonstrate caring for the poor. There are many other ways your family can practice caring, too.

63

Using a "Negative Brush"

It's easy for us adults to fall into the habit of speaking of certain neighborhoods as "bad areas." We may know what we mean, but for young children, "bad" has a specific, very negative meaning. Describing an area that way also tars all of the people there with the same, negative "brush." Most of us want our children to avoid those kind of gross generalizations about people and to treat them as individuals. So it's better to speak of "difficult places," "places where it's not easy to enjoy living," or "dangerous areas" instead.

Since our own concern for the poor is often based in our personal, spiritual and religious values, we can provide our children the same lasting foundation for that concern by sharing, as well as modeling, those values. Political and social values change rapidly and frequently, often at the prompting of an articulate politician or social upheaval. Only our demonstration of unchanging biblical values can be counted on to encourage children to make the world a more compassionate place and not to turn their hearts away from poverty, inequality, and injustice.[10]

That's quite a challenge, but highly successful parents understand and accept it. They know it's true "that a good child, more often than not, is the product of good parenting. Not perfect parenting, but guidance that reflects a sense of right and wrong, based on kindness, empathy and respect for others. That sounds like a tall order to me; it feels like one, too, as I try, day after day to be a good person so that I can be both a guide and a goad for my children."[11]

And how do successful parents become good persons for their children? By cultivating and deepening their own faith and obedience to God and seeking out advice and encouragement from trusted friends. It's work, but they do it because they're convinced there is no other way. *Good Parenting begins with Good Personing.*

Helping Children Cope With Materialism

One of the biggest challenges parents face today is helping their children develop a healthy attitude toward material *things*. Even the poorest of children are constantly bombarded each day with hours of skillful advertising designed to convince them that they just can't live without the latest clothing fad or electronic gadget. If you don't believe it's a problem, you've probably never taken a child on that annual expedition to shop for back-to-school clothes. It never fails. Shopping for clothing with children is invariably governed by two iron-clad laws. I've seen it happen over and over.

"The First Law of Childhood Clothing Selection" says that when your child has a choice between two perfectly good, apparently identical pieces of clothing, one costing at least twenty dollars more than the other, the child will choose the more expensive one every time-even if the price tags are hidden! I've tried arguing that the cheaper item looks just as good, but to no avail.

A second, related "law" applies especially to teenagers. It says that when faced with a choice between a "name brand" article of clothing or an apparently identical store brand, a teenager will always choose the name brand (and the higher price tag). Is there something the manufacturers do to those clothes that only eyes under the age of eighteen can detect? What's a concerned parent supposed to do?

Just Say No?

Shopping for new clothes can be either an exercise in diplomatic negotiations ("If you'll settle for this one, we'll go out for ice cream after") or an out and out power struggle ("Here are your choices. It's one of these or nothing!"). I've heard myself saying each of those lines at times.

65

When faced with a young son's plea for those $95 sneakers or a daughters request for another pair of designer jeans, reason often fails. (Remember Law #1?) Explaining that the $50 sneakers are just as well made as the other pair doesn't seem to matter. Reminding your daughter that she already has six pairs of those jeans doesn't settle anything. What's left? To just say "No!" and go home?

There are plenty of times when I just said "No!," but when that was all I said, I knew I hadn't taught my child much except who's the boss (and hopefully he already knew that!). Next I tried, "But we can't afford it now!" After all, that's often true and it did work for a while. But sooner or later our children discover the real truth: that we adults often can afford what we really **want** to afford.

Within limits, of course, we make choices about how to spend our money: how much to spend on a new car, whether to buy a new suit, how much to give to the Church. Every choice is a reflection of our values and priorities. Those values and priorities, in turn, reflect our spiritual decisions and commitments. So discussing these choices together (at levels appropriate to the ages of our children) is a good way to share your spiritual values with your children in a very concrete, practical way.

When my boys were young, they, like most young children, thought we could buy whatever we wanted. All it took was one of those magical things called "checks." So a request to buy a new bicycle (when the old one still worked well) gave us an opportunity to explain that God gave our family a certain amount of money. He promised to take care of all our needs but not necessarily all of our wants. We had to take care of our needs first; and they included giving to the Church and sharing with others. That was our first priority for spending our money. Then, with what was left, we could have at least some of our wants, too!

Of course, children and their parents don't always agree on the difference between needs and wants (We did buy the bicycle, although we had to wait a month or two)! I believe those conversations helped our sons learn that God does meet our needs while often supplying some of our wants, but that the proper priority for us is to put needs, including giving to God's work, first.

In order to reinforce this, our family has decided to try to avoid saying, "We can't afford it." Instead, we say something like, "We think there are other ways God would want us to spend our money" or "We have other priorities for our money right now" when discussing spending choices. That way, it's natural to talk with our children about what those "other priorities" and "ways to serve God with our money" really are.

Talking with your children about spending choices (in ways appropriate to their age, of course) is an effective way to introduce the concept of stewardship. Children don't need detailed information about family finances, but they do need to hear us explain and apply, as clearly as possible, the biblical values that shape our family spending choices. That way, God can develop those same values in them, too.

We try to avoid saying "we can't afford it" or referring to ourselves as "too poor" for another reason, also. God has blessed us too richly for us to speak that way, especially in contrast to other families in nearby inner-cities. "Not being able to afford it" communicates to children a feeling of dissatisfaction with never having enough. Instead, we want our children to learn the invaluable secret of contentment with all that they've been given by God. The Apostle Paul said, "Godliness with contentment is great gain."[12] Now that's certainly something that money can't buy!

Checking Our Own Closet

Moses taught the parents of Israel that they were first to be people of God themselves and then, by their daily example in family life, they would be able pass on their faith to their children.[13] Leading by example is the most powerful way successful parents shape the values of their children.

Leading by example in daily family life is not only a powerful, God-given parenting tool, it's also a very challenging one! Actions do speak louder than words. It's hard to explain to your daughter why she doesn't need that tenth pair of designer jeans if you have ten pairs in your closet, isn't it? It's hard to explain to your son why he doesn't need the latest electronic video game if all the latest, high-tech stereo and television equipment is staring at him from the den or family room. And it's hard to explain to our children why money can't buy happiness if it sure seems to do it for us.

More than once, I've been challenged by Jesus' words that "where your treasure is, there will your heart be, also."[14] For a few years, we lived next to a family that had a big boat. Every weekend during the summer they were off to the lake together. And every week when I wrote my check to the church, I thought "We could have a boat, too. Look at all the family fun we could have!"

I was disappointed with myself for those thoughts. It wouldn't take long for my sons to figure out that we'd be buying the boat with the money our family had previously given to the church. Wanting to be a highly successful parents has forced me to "check my own closet" once in a while. That way, I can see where my treasure and my heart really are—and so can my children.

Work It Out Daily

When things get quiet around our house, I can predict how my youngest son will respond. It happens about once a week. First, he gives out a loud cry of "I'm bored!" followed by "Can I go to the mall?" Going shopping is his first impulse when he has time on his hands.

68

Highly successful parents are convinced that helping children develop healthy habits toward material things is a full time, every day effort. Sometimes it involves fighting the urge to "go to the mall." That kind of family activity only "fans the flames" that we'd like to dampen! Better to use the time to do something together and build family relationships. Play a game, visit a nursing home, help a neighbor, cook a special meal together, take on a family project. Spend the time enjoying each other, not buying things. After all, which is more important?

Spending time enjoying each other, eating together, keeping in touch, openly sharing feelings of love and appreciation, and clearly communicating and demonstrating our faith and values are all ways parents truly help their children cope with the lure of materialism. These things build into children a sense of their self-worth that is so important to them as they grow up.

As we give them our love and share our faith and values, our children come to know who they are as our children and children of God. They grow to feel loved and accepted as a part of our family and the family of God. As they mature, they are gradually freed from an overwhelming need to have all the latest and most expensive toys in order to "fit in" or feel worthwhile.

Perhaps more importantly, living this way with and for our children demonstrates clearly what we believe and want them to know: that people, not possessions, are the most important things in life; that contentment is a choice you make, not a commodity you buy; that it's not what you wear but who you are that matters and that it's not what you have but what you do with it that pleases God. As children see their parents model those values consistently they are better able to resist the lure of "things."

My older son attended a college 350 miles from home and squarely in the country. Early on, he mentioned how he'd like to have a car to get around on weekends and to come home on breaks. I told him that I'd do what I could to help him buy one, but that there were some pressing family needs (including his tuition!) which also concerned me. "That's okay, Dad," he said. "Needs before wants. Let's keep our priorities straight!" That was a more mature response than I could have made at his age. I guess those childhood discussions we had about spending and priorities really did make a difference. They'll do the same for your children, too.

Service to Others

The first year, it was nothing more than just "a good thing to do." Since we didn't have any close family in the area to invite for Christmas dinner, our family decided to volunteer to help serve dinner at the city mission. We all had an assigned task. My wife and older son served the meals. Our younger son helped me set and clear tables. We worked hard for over two hours and were plenty tired when we left. But all of us, most especially my children, experienced first hand that day the joy of serving others—especially those less fortunate.

As we've continued that Christmas tradition over the years, my wife and I realized that we have had a number of family ministries of various types. We once opened our home to a young single man who needed a temporary home. We cared for a foster child for an extended period. We conducted vacation church schools in both resort and urban areas. My wife and I wanted to help our children develop caring and compassionate spirits and I believe that each of these ministries has helped nurture attitudes of caring and serving in our sons that have become a part of their personal identity as members of our family.

Ministries of hospitality are especially appealing to many families, since all but the youngest can actively participate. I'll always remember a family in the city where I went to college. I met them at church my freshman year.

70

They must have been able to tell I was a bit homesick and they invited me to have Sunday dinner with them and their children. When I arrived, I found a half dozen others from the campus there, too. Soon, it seemed we were going every Sunday.

If college students attend your church, you have a ready made guest list for a home cooked meal! And what international student could resist the offer of dinner at your home for a holiday celebration featuring your try at one of his native dishes? It's a great way to not only model service and hospitality for our children, but also to introduce them to new cultures and to clear their spirits of any seeds of prejudice and fear of people of different cultures or races.

Even a young child can help with hospitality by setting (or clearing) the table, making guest beds, or helping serve appetizers. Talk about your guests with your children before they arrive and try to guess what they might enjoy doing or talking about while visiting. That will help your children become sensitive to the needs of guests in the home.

One Memorable Ministry

One of our most memorable ministries came about when a family friend in his 30's needed a place to stay for a few months. Our small townhouse and its one bathroom were already crowded by the four of us, and we had to learn to accommodate our friend's nocturnal schedule. Our oldest son, seven at the time, shared his bedroom with our friend for those months—a practical act of giving and serving on his part.

A few years later, we took a foster daughter into our home for five years (from age 4-9). Having been abandoned by her mother twice before coming to us, she presented us all with many opportunities to learn and practice patience, understanding, forgiveness and love. With the exception of newborns, there are more children who need foster homes than there are homes to take them in. Taking a foster child is not for everyone, but there special rewards for those who serve in this way.

Children and the Elderly

Our society is aging, and nothing or no one brings a smile to the face and joy to the heart of many elderly folks than visit from children. It requires so little—the children only need be there and be themselves. We took our sons to visit relatives and friends in nursing homes when they were elementary school age. I was pleased that as a high school student, my older son chose to do his required community service by visiting shut-ins in a local nursing home! I'm not sure who got the most benefit from his efforts—him or the folks he visited! In any event, I know his nursing home experiences gave him a greater understanding and empathy for the elderly and the loneliness that often afflicts them.

Any ministries of hospitality do require some sacrifices, of course, but through them, our children can learn the joys of sensitively serving and putting the needs of others first. And serving along with us (following our example) is the most effective way to learn those vital lessons.

Do as I Say...

He was just a little boy, about six years old. He had just returned from Sunday School, and his father watched as he emptied his pockets. There was a new box of crayons, a shiny pair of scissors, and two new pencils. The father knew the family hadn't bought those objects so he asked his son suspiciously "Where did you get those?." "I took them from Sunday School," the boy answered. At that, his father let loose with an angry harangue. "How could you? Haven't I told you not to take things that aren't yours? Don't you know that's stealing? If you wanted them, all you had to do was ask me and I'd have brought them home for you from the office."

The old adage "Actions Speak Louder Than Words" was never more clearly demonstrated. Highly successful parents are convinced that a "do as I say" approach won't work in developing spiritual values with children unless it's matched by a "do as I do" approach. That father expressed certain values with his lips, but his life said something totally different. Which method do you suppose had the greatest impact on his son?

Jack and Judy Baliswick, who are both parents and university professors, describe different styles of parenting according to the amount of content taught as well as the modeling of those values that takes place. What they label a "neglecting" style of parenting neither "practices" (models) nor "preaches" (verbally teaches) desired behavior.

The "teaching" style, on the other hand, is high in content taught verbally (it "preaches," teaches, and explains) but low in actual "practice" of those attitudes and values (modeling or demonstrating of the desired behavior). Children parented by this model may feel "preached at," which is very counter-productive with teenagers!

The "modeling" style, the Baliswick's point out, is a definite improvement over the previous two. It is high on action (practice) but low on teaching and explanation. Parents do model desired behavior, but they don't explain it. The children see proper behavior demonstrated, but then they have to try to figure out for themselves the values underlying why parents act as they do.

The most complete and successful parenting style is what the Baliswicks call "Discipling." It is high in both "practice" (modeling) and "preaching" (verbal teaching and explaining). This is clearly the most effective in training children in desired behavior.[15] Highly successful parents teach both by word **and** deed. They disciple their children by "practicing what they (also) preach."

Use Everyday Situations

Even the ancients recognized the critical role parents play in guiding the spiritual development of their children. And they also knew how critical parents' examples are in that process. Today, also, successful parents prepare to pass their spiritual and moral values to their children by examining their own values and determining how central a part they play in their own lives.

The biblical teacher Moses told his people to "impress" certain values on their children. In other words, they were to teach these values to their children in such a way that the values left a lasting mark, an impression, on their children's lives. But in order to do this, Moses said, parents must first impress these values on their own hearts. Their own lives must bear the mark of these values before they can impress them on their children. Then, the children can come to share their parent's faith.[16]

That's another way of expressing the central conviction of highly successful parents mentioned earlier— *Good Parenting begins with Good Personing.* Successful parents aren't perfect, but they do their best to model for their children the faith and values they want their children to have, and they keep working to be the best models they can be!

Successful parents use all the everyday situations of family life—even the most mundane—to teach moral values. Values such as honestly, fidelity, love of God and respect for others are passed to our children in the give and take of daily family life as they watch our example. If we don't have it in us—if it's not impressed on our hearts—we can't give it to our children.

Learning from My Father

The same principle applies to spiritual values and practices. For example, what do you tell your children about the importance of prayer, Bible reading, and attending church? Do you tell them that the Bible is God's word, the most important book in the world? How often and how seriously do they see you reading it? Do you tell your children that prayer is their lifeline to their heavenly Father? That God hears and answers prayer? How often and how seriously do they hear you talking on that lifeline? Do you help them learn to bring their cares to the one who invites them to cast all their anxiety on him because he cares for them?[17] Do you tell your children that God loves and values everyone equally? Do they hear you tell "ethnic jokes" or refer disparagingly to poor people or people of a different race or faith?

Don't get me wrong. Actions do speak louder than words, but words **are** important. As our children get older, they need to hear us express and explain what we believe so that they can understand and accept those values as they grow.

In another book, *It's The Little Things That Count*,[18] I told how my father helped me see how easily and naturally we can share our faith and values with our children. He and my mother had come to visit one weekend. Dad, my two sons, and I got up early that Saturday to go out for breakfast. We all piled into our little Chevette. It was a foggy morning, so I turned on the lights as we drove to the restaurant. Of course, I forgot to turn them off while we were eating, and, when we came out an hour later, the battery was dead.

Neither Dad nor I knew what to do. It looked like we'd have to call my wife to come and rescue us. But just then, out of the restaurant came a man who offered to help. Our car was standard shift, and he knew just how to roll it down the little grade in the parking lot to start it. As we were on our way home, my dad said "Wasn't that good of

God to send that man to help us!" It certainly was. And it was good of Dad to say that so that my sons could recognize this example of God's care for us.

"I'm glad God helped you not be nervous on that test today." "Isn't it great that God helped Jimmy get better, just like we prayed"? "Wasn't God good to send that man to help us!" Highly successful parents are convinced that expressing their faith this way before their children helps them see God's activity in the life of their family and others. Doing so enables children to develop the "spiritual eyes" necessary to recognize his presence and care in their own lives.

Stones that Speak

Stones come in all sorts of shapes and sizes and weights. Some are very beautiful. Some, such as gems, are precious. But who ever heard of stones that speak? Yet, in a way, they do. Ancient stones unearthed by archaeologists or geologists tell secrets of the earth thousands of years ago. Memorial stones in cemeteries tell of the lives of men and women who once lived and breathed like you and I.

As a parent, one of my favorite Bible passages is Joshua, Chapter 4. There, the story is told of Joshua, who succeeded Moses, as the leader of the people of Israel. His job was to finally lead them into the Promised Land. Only one obstacle stood in the way—the Jordan River. It was very deep and very wide. And no one had any boats. How would they get across? God took care of it by parting the Jordan just as he had parted the Red Sea when Israel fled out of Egypt. The people crossed on dry land.

Then, God told Joshua to have one man from each of the twelve tribes of the nation pick up one stone from the river bed and take it with them into the promised land. God knew that sooner or later, the children, in their natural curiosity, would notice the stones and ask "What do these stones mean?" Then, the parents would tell them the story of how God had acted in power to help them and how he had kept his promise to them. As concrete reminders of God's powerful care for His people those stones clearly "spoke" important words to the Israelite children.

As parents, our lives are like stones that speak to our children. As we live our faith consistently before our children, we provoke their natural curiosity. They watch us as we go about our daily lives and are always asking "What do these stones mean? Why do you act that way, Mom? Why do we believe that, Dad? Is God real? Can I really trust him to care for me?" One of the greatest privileges we parents have is to be heroes and models for our children—stones that speak to them of the everyday reality of God's faithfulness and love. What does **your** stone say?

Highly successful parents are guided by the fundamental conviction that *Good Parenting begins with Good Personing*. The key to successful parenting does not lie in how much education we have, whether our temperaments match those of our children, or whether we follow the right "experts." The key is found in who we are and who we are becoming. As the old saying goes "The acorn doesn't fall far from the tree." So, how healthy is your tree?

Chapter 4

Two Heads are Better Than One

One of the main issues of debate in the 1992 presidential campaign was family values. The flashpoint of the debate came when a popular TV character named Murphy Brown became pregnant and decided she didn't need to marry the child's father. Both she and the child would do just fine without him. She chose unwed motherhood instead.

While some critics hailed this as breaking new ground for women's rights, others saw it from a very different perspective: the child's. In a major campaign speech, then-Vice President Dan Quayle denounced Murphy Brown's decision. Children need fathers as well as mothers, Quayle argued. Two parent families are better for both the child and society. They should be encouraged whenever possible.

For the remainder of the campaign, Quayle was ridiculed as narrow minded and unfair to single mothers. But it wasn't long before a flood of articles in the media concluded that, in the words of the *Atlantic Monthly*, "Dan Quayle Was Right."[1] "The social science evidence is in," the article proclaimed, "though it may benefit the adults involved, the dissolution of intact, two-parent families is harmful to large numbers of children."[2]

A virtual epidemic of divorce and unwed motherhood has swept our country in recent decades. It is clear that "if current trends continue, less than half of all children born today will live continuously with their own mother and father throughout childhood. Most American children will spend several years in a single mother family."[3]

The harm caused children by the decline of two parent families is as depressing as it is clear. Compared to intact, two-parent families, children in single parent families are six times as likely to be poor and stay poor. They are two to three times as likely to have emotional and behavioral problems. They are at greater risk for sexual abuse. And overall, they're more likely to be unsuccessful and unhappy as adults, "particularly in the domains of life, love and work, that are most essential to happiness."[4] The evidence shows that Murphy Brown was wrong and Dan Quayle was, indeed, right. Children need both parents—their fathers as well as their mothers.

Two parent families also benefit the parents. It is true that successful parenting is hard work, but it's much easier and more rewarding when you share it with a loving spouse. The writer of the book of Ecclesiastes summed up this ancient wisdom this way: "Two are better than one, because they have a good reward for their toil. For if they fall, one will lift up the other; but woe to one who is alone and falls and does not have another to help."[5]

..Until the Day I Die

When you introduce yourself to someone, what do you say? I usually say something like "Hello, I'm Rich Patterson. I'm a clergyman and writer." After our name, most of us (especially men) identify ourselves primarily by our occupation.

In my case, and perhaps in yours too, our occupation doesn't tell who we really are. If I wanted to tell you that,

I'd say "Hello, I'm Rich Patterson. I'm a husband and father. My occupations are clergyman and writer." You see, I've discovered that, after almost 30 years of marriage and nearly that long as a parent, what's most important to me is my marriage and children. *I'm a husband and a father first, and I wouldn't have it any other way.*

Sara and I have two sons. One has graduated from college and is living on his own. His brother will soon be off to college, too, and then our active parenting days will be over. Then, I'll make the same adjustment to my sons that my father made to me: from "father in charge" to "father friend." Our relationship will change, but I'll still be their father. In fact, I don't ever want to stop being a father. It's too great a source of happiness and satisfaction for me. I agree completely with another father who said, "If I live to be 90, I want to be a dad all the way until I die."[6]

Of course, I didn't become a father alone! Sara and I were married and became parents *together*. In 1971, friends who predicted that we'd grow tired of each other or become strangers living in the same house and get divorced could easily have been right. But it hasn't worked out that way. We began our marriage committed to each other and to any children God gave us. We've worked hard over the years to keep our marriage and our parenting partnership strong.

It hasn't been easy, but, as the writer of Ecclesiastes observed, now we "have a good reward for our toil." Believe it or not, after all these years, Sara and I still enjoy each other's company. We still look forward to our annual vacation and the opportunity to spend time together walking on the beach, riding our bikes or just sitting together quietly and reading. By the grace of God, our children have two parents; a mother *and* a father! I wish no less for every child!

Unfortunately, that's not always the way it works out for children. As we've seen, only about half of children today spend their entire childhood in an intact family. Since most single parents are mothers, many children don't get to grow up with their fathers in the home. These children don't benefit from daily, intimate relationships with their fathers. Is this a serious problem? Apart from the (serious) financial and discipline issues, what difference does it really make in the long run? After all, these children do have caring, nurturing mothers. Can't their **mothers** give them everything they need? Or is there something children need that only fathers can give?

Not Just "Assistant Mothers"

I haven't been a perfect father by any means but I have tried to be actively involved in the day to day raising of our two sons. I, too, have vivid memories of waiting for news of their births, of toilet training, early school days, adolescence, and drivers licenses.

I've tried to give them everything I could: time and attention, love and limits, kindness and firmness, encouragement and values, spiritual training and most of all, the best example I could provide. And besides me, their mother has had a tremendous impact on them. I believe our children will be happier, more successful adults because both of us were actively, intimately, and daily involved in parenting them. Whatever measure of success God gives us will be the result of this parenting partnership.

But today, not everyone believes this. In some circles, fathers are under serious attack. In his landmark book, *Fatherless America*, David Blankenhorn says plainly that "Men in general and fathers in particular, are increasingly viewed as superfluous to family life; either as expendable or as part of the problem." Fathers are superfluous because, in the opinion of many experts, there "are not, and ought not to be, any key parental tasks that belong essentially and primarily to fathers."[7] Does every child need a father? Our society increasingly answers "no," or at least "not necessarily."[8]

And this is one case where many families are "practicing what they preach." As of 1990, over 1/3 of all children in this country lived apart from their biological father.[9] By 1992, over 20% of families with children were headed by mothers. Of children of divorce, 1/2 have never even visited their fathers house![10] How involved together can these children and fathers be?

The view that fathers really aren't necessary to the successful raising of children is growing in acceptance— especially in feminist circles. To them, men are "the problem." They beat and oppress women (and children, too). The solution is to remove from the definition of fatherhood any and every facet that might be exclusively or even primarily male. Then, "fathers" can be turned into "mothers" in every sense except the biological.

In the musical "My Fair Lady," Prof. Henry Higgins asked, "Why can't a woman be more like a man?" Some feminists and other "experts" have turned that question on its head and they ask "Why can't a father be more like a mother?" When this androgynous parenthood is finally realized, they feel maleness will disappear and will finally allow for the greatest degree of human (especially female!) freedom and fulfillment.[11]

But highly successful parents are convinced that two parents are better than one. They believe children would be the big losers of this "gender convergence" because all the wonderful and unique gifts that loving fathers give their children every day would be lost. Fathers—unnecessary? That flies in the face of both common sense and the experience of human families for untold centuries. Children need both parents—mothers and **fathers, too.**

What's So Special about Fathers, Anyway?

In fact, some expert voices are beginning to speak up on behalf of fathers. Nationally syndicated columnist David

Broder notes that study and discussion groups across the political and social spectrum have agreed that "our children are in worse shape than generally thought as a result of having been victimized by certain cultural trends, particularly the rise in divorce and illegitimacy" both of which tend to deprive children of their fathers.[12]

As this fragile, common sense consensus emerges, experts are beginning to re-examine why it is that children need their fathers. What are the particular contributions to parenting that fathers make? How are fathers different from mothers? What is it about fathering that makes it more than just an "instant replay" of mothering?

Recent research shows how much fathers contribute to their children's development right from the beginning. Children whose fathers are actively involved with them while they were infants tend to be more successful with friends, school, and dealing with emotions later in life. One study found that "when fathers regularly talked, played, soothed, fed, and changed their babies during the first month of life, the children scored significantly higher on developmental tests of motor skills, pattern identification, word recognition and problem solving at age 1."[13]

When they were preschoolers, our sons both enjoyed wrestling on the living room floor with me. Their mother would always hover over us with a worried look on her face saying things like "Stop that. You'll hurt them. Be careful!" But we'd go right on wrestling. To me, it was part of their birthright as boys!

In fact, research shows that fathers play more physically with their children than mothers do. "Rough-housing" is a normal part of father-play. "Father-play tends to be lively, unpredictable, creative, imaginative, and obviously exciting." Children go to Mom for warm, quiet activities and serious talk. Is it any wonder children often prefer to play with their fathers?[14]

Even in the earliest weeks of a baby's life, a father benefits them by relating to them differently than a mother.

Fathers tend to "play more physical games and talk to their children more often in adult tones than mothers." According to Dr. Brad Sachs, director of The Father Center in Columbia, Maryland, "Fathers exercise aspects of the infant—stimulating different muscle groups and parts of the brain, and ways of integrating the two—that might be benignly neglected if a child were cared for solely by a woman."[15]

In this case, successful parents, the experts, and common sense all agree: children need their fathers. The different styles that fathers and mothers bring to parenting are both crucial to a child's development. They each teach a child something different, or something from a different perspective, about life. Dr. T. Barry Brazelton feels that "each parent offers an entirely different model for the baby so each fosters a different side of the baby's personality."[16] And in order to have a fully developed personality, and be fully human, children need what fathers offer.

A Whole Different Perspective

As any mother knows, fathers approach parenting from a whole different perspective than do most mothers. Susan Reimer, a writer for the *Baltimore Sun*, illustrates this humorously from her own experience.

One night, she called home from work at 10:30 p.m. and was surprised to find that the children were still awake. When she asked why, her husband replied "We're playing strip poker. They didn't want to get undressed for bed so I told them we were going to play strip poker and when they got down to their underwear they had to go to bed." It's obvious, Reimer says, "that men don't share the standards we relentless mothers have established. I rent *My Fair Lady* and *West Side Story* to watch with my children. I talk about the origin of musical theater and the themes of race and class prejudice. My husband rents *Spaceballs* and he and the kids curl up under the afghan and laugh like crazy."[17] Fathers bring a whole new approach to parenting than do mothers, and children who get to enjoy them both are happier because of it!

Fathers also often help promote a sense of adventure and independence (and resulting self-confidence) in their children that is valuable later in life. When our oldest son was fifteen, he had an opportunity to go to Jamaica for two weeks. His mother's first thoughts were of all the dangers and problems he'd face (most were quite real!). My first reaction was to think that this was a tremendous opportunity to learn and to practice to be independent (then, I thought of all the dangers!). Once again, we saw how men and women parent differently. Each has something important to add to the parenting recipe. Loving, involved fathers make their own valuable and unique contributions to a child's growth and development.

Kent State Psychologist John Guidibaldi led an eleven-year study of almost 700 families in 38 states. He found that the unique contributions of fathers to parenting were in the areas of discipline and control, role modeling, and the transmission of values.[18] If your experience as a father (or with your own father) is like mine, you can see that his conclusions do make sense.

Today we hear a lot fewer cries of "Wait until your father gets home!" but fathers often still take significant responsibility for discipline and control, especially over adolescent boys. And when the father is absent from the home, studies show that children, especially adolescents, tend toward greater discipline and behavior problems.[19] Divorce and unwed motherhood have robbed many children of daily parenting by their fathers, and the result is children at risk of depression, lower self-esteem and less academic success.[20]

Here's how one wise father (who's also a family psychologist) described the important contributions of a father to his children:

Your children need you. They need your attention, your encouragement, your wisdom, your physical contact, your affirmation of how important they are to you." In fact, he says, "there is no one in the whole world who has the power and potential influence to help your child feel better about himself than you."[21]

Attention, encouragement, wisdom, affirmation and affection; highly successful fathers give all these to their children. They hug and cuddle, kiss and feed, change and comfort their children, just as mothers do. And they do all the other mundane things that nurture implies: managing the household, taking the kids to the doctor, even washing the dishes! Nurturing fathers are not junior, but full partners in parenting with their wives. They carry their part of the parenting load, not because they have to, but because they want to.[22]

As a result, their children are the richer in many ways. According to Dr. Kyle Pruett of the Yale Medical School, children whose fathers are involved in their care and nurture are themselves more nurturing and generative. A twenty-six year study of parental involvement with children also showed that the father's influence in producing children who become compassionate and empathetic "was quite astonishing." Boys who are raised with warm, nurturing fathers grow up to become more socially adept and self-confident.[23]

Highly successful parents are convinced that fathers are invaluable role models for their children. Fathers..."your children need your wisdom. As a role model, you will teach them how to be in the world. You will provide a source of values. Your sons and daughters need you to provide them with a healthy image of a man-your son, so he can follow in your footsteps and your daughter, so she will choose a good person for future romantic involvement."[24]

Single mothers often realize that their sons needs this male role model. So, they turn to grandfathers, uncles or other male friends to fill the need. Others enroll their sons in Boys Scouts, Big Brothers or organized sports to give them male role models. They may even read their sons biographies of great men such as Martin Luther King, Jr. or Abraham Lincoln.[25]

But successful parents realize that girls need their fathers as much as boys need them. The evidence from social science "suggests that fatherless boys tend toward disorderly and violent behavior" and that "fatherless girls tend toward personally and socially destructive relationships with men" including "early sexual activity and unmarried motherhood."[26]

A study of nearly 1000 families with children 5-18 years old conducted by a sociologist at the University of Nebraska found that "the more time dads say they spend with kids and the more supportive their relationship, the fewer behavioral problems" the children had. And another study showed that "girls with involved fathers are more likely to delay sex and less likely to use drugs or alcohol." The same positive effects were also observed regarding the involvement of step-dads and dads in divorced families.[27] So, research is confirming it: dads are vital to their children's healthy growth and development. Dads do make a difference!

Children Want Their Fathers, Too!

It does make sense, doesn't it? God must have given children fathers for good reasons! Good conduct, academic achievement, self-esteem, psychological health, social relationships, overall economic well being, and spiritual maturity, are all endangered when a loving father is not able to parent his child. So we fathers can relax. We really are needed! And children do want their fathers! Nearly ten percent of all children born today are born to mothers who deliberately choose single motherhood.[28] But, as David

Blankenhorn relates poignantly, children miss and mourn even fathers they've never known.

Blankenhorn tells of one unmarried mother who had carefully planned exactly what she'd say to her son when he asked about his father. She'd say it really didn't matter and anyway, that he had a host of adult friends and relatives to make up for it. But by the time he was three, her son was obsessed with fathers—especially everyone else's. His day care worker told his mother how "Sam has been telling all the other kids' daddies that he doesn't have a daddy, and he says it very sadly when they come to pick up their children."[29]

Another single-mother-by-choice thought that "if I had a child and I was the one raising him and I was a good parent, it would make absolutely no difference there not being a father in the house—that the child wouldn't miss it. That was before I had Keith." The child loved his father and, though they saw each other regularly, he still clearly missed having his father around daily.[30]

Girls miss their fathers, too. Author Richard Louv tells of one troubled teenage girl named Linda. One day, she swore at a teacher and was assigned to detention after school When she walked in the door at home, she hadn't even put her things down, when her dad came after her. He beat her, punched her in the lip and slammed her head against the wall. Still, she loves her dad and doesn't want to be separated from him. "I love my dad to death, but I hate him. I don't know what I'd do if he died. I'd freak out, because he's my dad." This abuse is absolutely inexcusable. But, Linda's statement speaks to the significant role and influence fathers have in their children's lives.[31]

Fathers as Protectors

Once when my youngest son was eleven, he was enjoying his first day with a young boy's most precious possession—a new bike. He rode it to a friend's house and left it on the lawn. When he came out, it had been stolen. He came home in tears and I did what any father would do. I got in the car and drove around the neighborhood until we spotted a boy riding a bike just like my son's. When I confronted him, he couldn't explain where he got it or whose it was, so I repossessed it, put it in the trunk of the car, and took it home. Protection. Children need it. Fathers give it.

The protector role that fathers play for their children goes beyond just physical protection. Fathers also protect their children from the destructive forces of modern society. I only had to watch MTV once to know that I wanted to protect my sons from its harmful, degrading influence. The Internet, still largely unregulated, presents similar dangers. What parent hasn't wished they could somehow shield their children from the effects of pornography, sexual license, indifference to life, greed, materialism, and a host of other social ills?

I can't shield my children from all the destructive influences around them, but I can prepare them to recognize and deal with those forces successfully. Just as importantly, I can work to alleviate them. Not all of us enjoy working in the political arena, but if you are willing to write letters to politicians, sponsor petitions to school boards, and vote, you can help alleviate some of the worst effects of pornography, indifference to life, and the erosion of parental authority and family friendly social values. Support organizations that support things that make for a healthier future for your children and grandchildren. That's another important way fathers (and mothers!) protect their children.

We can't turn back the clock, but we can also protect our children by preparing them for living in an uncertain and dangerous future. Fathers teach and instill the values and attitudes their children will need to live successfully in the world when they are adults. When I was first married, I enjoyed a glass of wine now and then. But when my boys began to reach elementary years, I decided not to have any alcohol in the house. There's too much pain and destruction in our society today caused by misuse of alcohol. I hoped I could help protect them from that by my example.

Other times, I've decided against renting certain videos that I wanted to watch. It wasn't easy, but I knew that I wanted to teach my sons, by my words and example, to give their attention to "whatever is true, whatever is honorable, whatever is just, whatever is pure, whatever is pleasing, whatever is commendable," whatever is excellent, and whatever is praiseworthy.[32] That will nurture their spirits, and protect and prepare them for successful adulthood in spite of the dangerous world in which they live.

The Most Essential Task

In fact, this may be "the most essential task of modern fatherhood." David Blankenhorn calls it "paternal cultural transmission" or "sponsorship" of our children. In plain language, it's teaching them how to live, "endowing children with competence and character by showing them how to lead a certain way of life."[33] It's what we've called discipleship.

Don't mothers do this, too? Of course they do. Often mothers focus their efforts on the important emotional and relational aspects of life (being kind, caring and sharing, etc.). Fathers often concentrate on preparing their children for the future, on developing qualities such as "independence, self-reliance, and the willingness to test limits and take risks" (things mothers aren't always so keen on!).[34] *Highly successful parents are convinced that children need both emphases; that here, as in many areas of life, "two heads are better than one."*

When fathers talk to our children about fair play on the ball field, about getting along in school, and about the worth of honesty, integrity, and faith, they shape and mold their children's spirits and character for all their adult lives.

This is the real difference between biological paternity and fatherhood. "The former helps to produce a child. The latter helps to produce an adult."[35]

Of course, at the heart of teaching our children a way of living is promoting their spiritual growth. There's no substitute for a father's role in the spiritual formation of his children. Recently, I spoke with a mother now in her 60's. She has two sons, both are grown. She expressed her disappointment that they were not more deeply committed to the Christian faith. "But their father never really took the lead in seeing that they went to church or in teaching them the faith. At the time, he wasn't mature enough himself," she said.

It happens over and over, especially with boys. The mother tries hard to instill a vital faith in her children. Still, it's as if the child decides, "If it's not good enough for my father, it's not good enough for me." That just seems like common sense to a child. It's no coincidence that, from ancient times, fathers as well as mothers have been urged to give spiritual instruction to their children.[36]

Teaching his children "a way of life" is a father's priceless contribution to the developing character of his children. As divorce and unmarried motherhood spreads fatherlessness, it's no surprise that children are growing up with a serious "characterological deficit." It results in increased juvenile violence, especially among boys, and the high teen age pregnancy rates.[37] Of course, mothers help shape their children's character, too. But when fathers aren't there to make their unique contribution, children suffer.

Let's be bold enough to say it: *God gave children both a mother and a father for good and loving reasons. Children are a two-parent project.* When it comes to parenting, fathers are not a luxury. They're special and they're needed—especially when it comes to shaping the spiritual lives of their children.

Reflecting God's Character to Our Children

As a new parent, I read every parenting book I could find! I was determined to be the best possible father any child could have! As a Christian, I prayed for God's guidance frequently because I had read that more than just my children's future emotional health was at stake. I knew that my parenting would inevitably shape the spiritual lives of my children.

All the books I read told me that children form their first, most lasting impressions of the character of God from their early interactions with their parents. My wife and I realized that, in a very real sense, we represented God to our infant sons. I must admit that was frightening. What would our children learn about God? How accurately would they experience his love and care as a result of our parenting? Being good parents seemed like an almost impossible task. But, over the quarter century since then, God has graciously taught, guided, and corrected me as I have struggled to reflect his character with integrity to my children.

Children are "Others"

"Stop acting like a baby and get over here right now!" My tone of voice was harsh and my sharp words mocked my four year-old son's tears. Even as I shouted them, I didn't feel right. " Parents talk to their children this way most of the time," I said to myself. "It's no big problem." But no matter what other parents did, I knew my words and my tone of voice didn't reflect God's love for my son—or my love either! After some prayer, I realized that I had been violating one of God's basic rules of human relationships: "Do unto others as you would have them do to you."[38] The "Golden Rule" is not just meant to govern adult relationships—it applies to children, also. Specifically, I believe it applies to parent-child relationships.

Surely, children are among those "others" who deserve to be treated with the same honor and respect that we parents expect (even demand) for ourselves. It is enough that Christ commands it, but he also holds up our children as spiritual examples.[39] For that reason also, children deserve the respect and honor of all adults, especially their parents. I knew that, but often, like many other parents, I didn't act accordingly!

The tone of voice I used with my sons was better suited to a military setting than a home where the parents wanted to reflect God's character. One of their Heavenly Father's most gracious gifts is the dignity and value he has given them as those who share in his image and benefit from his constant love and care. God intended them to receive that gift through my wife and me, and my habit of speaking so gruffly was interfering with delivery of that gift!

This is a problem that has plagued other parents. I know of one mother who had the habit of barking out orders to her children ("Clean the table now!") like a drill sergeant to new recruits, much as I had done. Then one day, her supervisor at work spoke to her harshly in front of the entire office. She felt both angry and ashamed. Later, it occurred to her that her children might have the same feelings when she spoke to them that way. After that, she, too, resolved to be guided by the Golden Rule when speaking to her children.

Scripture advises us not to "let any unwholesome talk come out of your mouths, but only what is helpful for building others up according to their needs, that it may benefit those who listen."[40] Those words also apply to children. Their tender, young spirits need to be encouraged and built up, especially by those God has placed closest to them—their parents. Yet these tenders spirits are still learning about the wonder of God's unconditional love for them and are easily bruised and torn by careless and harsh language. "How could you be such a klutz?" "Stop being such a cry baby!" More than once, I've prayed for forgiveness for letting my words mar my child's vision of God's love for him!

But What about Reprimands?

Treating our children with honor and respect does not mean that we neglect to discipline or reprimand them, even severely at times. When a reprimand is necessary, we dishonor our children and distort the character of God's love by refusing to give it.

The biggest challenge I faced was to discipline in a way that reflected God's loving, redemptive discipline of his children. It's so easy to discipline or correct in a way that is humiliating to a child! But respect for a child's dignity and feelings (to say nothing of love) means avoiding humiliating them, as much as possible. So, intentional humiliation has no place in our discipline, for it is not loving. Rather than delighting in exposing our sin and failure, God's love "covers a multitude of sins," seeking to shelter our sins and failures from the mocking gazes of others.[41]

I remember the humiliation (and anger) I felt as a child being spanked in front of my siblings. It's usually quite possible to carry out such discipline in the bedroom where prying eyes can not see. It is when your child needs serious correction while visiting another home, attending worship, eating out, or shopping at the mall that our love goes the extra mile in order to avoid humiliation. Private homes have bedrooms or bathrooms to which you can retreat (and in which your child can remain until fully recovered). Most public buildings also have bathrooms or out-of-the-way corners that provide a measure of privacy. Is it more work to discipline this way? Of course. But what better reflects to our children the **loving** discipline of their Heavenly Father?

Discipline is Discipling

It's clear that disciplining our children in a Godly way is no easy job, especially since, for many of us, the very word "discipline" brings to mind mostly unpleasant times of correction and reprimand. But "discipline" is closely related to the word "disciple." And, as we'll discuss in some detail in chapter seven, Christian discipline is, first of all, a positive process of discipling. Its goal is that our children grow into mature disciples of Christ. So we "show and tell" them what that means. We parents are disciples of Jesus Christ who say to our children "Follow my example, as I follow the example of Christ."[42]

That's why it's so important that I treat my children with all the dignity and respect possible. Nobody—child or adult—is a willing disciple of someone whom they do not respect. If my sons are to "Follow my example, as I follow the example of Christ," I must build mutual respect between us. Once again, the wisdom of God's laws is apparent. Treating my children according to the Golden Rule is not just right, but also wise Christian parenting!

In Chapter 2, I told you about our foster daughter, Antoinette, who lived with us for five years. She came from a neglectful family background. Years later, I look back and see a five year-old girl who never felt as if she mattered to anyone, never felt as if she had any control over her life, never felt any dignity or self-worth. And she was always testing me, testing our limits. My relationship with her was one power struggle after another. I managed to "win" most of the time, but in reality, we both lost. My attempts to show her who was boss and to be sure she learned her lesson just made her more angry, frustrated and convinced she was unlovable and unloved. They certainly did not create a relationship reflecting God's love and were not conducive to discipling!

Preserving A Child's Dignity

I've since learned a lot about the value of avoiding unnecessary power struggles when disciplining (and discipling) my children. No one above the age of two or three enjoys (or benefits from) always being given orders. God created us to want and need appropriate degrees of freedom and choices in order to grow and mature. Many times, conflicts can be avoided and a child's dignity preserved simply by giving them age and situation appropriate choices and responsibility.

For example, instead of a confrontation over an order to "clean up your room this minute," the choice to clean it up now or right after dinner can avoid unnecessary conflicts. And no one enjoys being given an order and then having someone stand over them with a grim look, watching until it's done. That's humiliating. It's kinder and more "face-saving" to say, "I'll check back in a few minutes and see how your room cleaning is coming," and then leave.

We went through the battles of young children wanting to choose their own clothes, even in the heat of summer or cold of winter. Preschool children who insist on choosing their own clothes can be given a choice between two sets (that you've pre-chosen). That way, everybody wins. You teach (disciple) a good clothing choice, and the child's dignity and your discipling relationship are both enhanced.

The same principle has helped us with our teens, also. When my sons were sixteen, I began to ask "When do you expect to be home?" instead of first setting a curfew. If I liked the answer I got, we were both happy. "Alright, I'll expect to see you then," I said. "Have a great time." They had not been given a curfew. They had chosen their own. If I didn't like their answer, we'd negotiate.

Choices and responsibility avoid power struggles. Ultimately, nobody wins if your parenting is a continual series of power struggles. Jesus didn't base his discipling on power (although he could have). Disciplining is ultimately based on love and respect. Avoiding power struggles when possible and affirming the dignity of children by allowing them appropriate choices builds them up and encourages them. It reflects the loving character of God as he disciples us.

God is a "Yes" Parent

I believe that God, my father, wants to give me the desires of my heart—and more! Although, in his love, he cannot give me everything I ask, I believe it gives him great pleasure when he can say "Yes" to my requests. Any loving parent would feel the same way. So as I work to reflect God's loving character to my children, I try to be a "Yes" parent. My personal rule is to try to say "Yes" to my children *unless there is a good reason not to do so.* This is very different from saying "no" unless they can somehow convince me.

I admit is a hard rule to follow. When I get tired, the first word out of my mouth is usually "No." My child's request often comes at a very inconvenient time. And sometimes, there really is a good reason to say "No." But often, I say "No" just because I don't want to be bothered right then. How thankful I am that God doesn't answer my prayers that way! He doesn't look for the convenient way. He isn't bothered by my requests. He's ready to listen and respond in love, respectful of my desires and needs. God is a "Yes" parent, and I want to be one, too.

Being a "Yes" parent has some practical benefits. Saying "Yes" unless there is a good reason not to do so, instead of an automatic "No," reduces the occasions for whining and nagging. And when I do have to say "No," my children understand that I'm serious because I don't do it unless there is a good reason. They may not be happy, but they understand my "No" is a reflection of my love. In the same way, while we may not always appreciate or understand God's good reason for saying "No," we are convinced of his love because he so often says "Yes" even before we ask! As a "Yes parent," I want to model that aspect of God's loving character to my children.

The Greatest Lesson

Over nearly 25 years as a father, I have learned many lessons from studying how God parents me, and I think I've finally learned how to be the best father possible: by personally striving to know God, my heavenly "parent," by growing closer to Him daily, and by letting his Holy Spirit make me more and more into his image. That way, a little of his perfect parenting can begin to be reflected to my children through me!

Experiencing my own deep, fierce love for my children, has given me a glimpse into God's love for me. Perhaps that's the greatest lesson I've learned from parenting. And how glad I am that even though I'm an adult, God will always be, in a very real sense, my parent. I'm still experiencing his gracious parental love and discipline, and I'm learning yet more of his perfect and gracious character. Being a Christian parent has been a quarter-century spiritual education for me! And there's so much more yet to learn! I can't bear to stop now!

Perhaps that's why I'm so thankful that, although my sons are mostly grown, I'll always be their father. Soon, I won't be disciplining them anymore, but I'll always be discipling them. That's good news! So there's added incentive to keep striving to know God better and to keep looking for new ways to reflect God's character to them. I guess I've learned that an ever-growing disciple who disciples his children really is the best father any child could have! And a very, very valuable part of God's plan for their physical, emotional, and spiritual growth and development.

I Just Wish I Knew How

"I really want to be a better father, but I'm not sure how." I've heard that lament from many fathers as I've traveled across the country. Their father wasn't a great model. He worked hard, provided economically for his family, and handled the hardest discipline problems. That was the sum of his fathering. How's his son supposed to know how to do any better?

If you're a father who wants to be the best father you can be (or a mother who wants to encourage her husband), here are five simple strategies to follow. They've worked for me and countless other fathers. I know they'll help you, too. Notice that they all have one important thing in common: a willingness to learn.

1. <u>Learn from your wife.</u>

By now you know that I don't mean to just copy her style. Your children don't need you to become an assistant mother! Remember that God gave children two parents— two *different* parents. There are many things we fathers can learn from our wives, however.

Learn to Listen. Women often discern feelings more quickly than men do. When our children tell us about what they've done or what has disappointed them, we are quick to offer an analysis of the situation or a solution. Watch how your wife listens not only to what your child says, but to what they feel. First, listen to their feelings and get in touch with their heart as well as their head. Then you can offer the full range of gifts that successful fathers give their children: encouragement, affirmation and guidance.

Learn Patience. As we've seen, one of the valuable contributions that fathers offer children is positive discipline and control. But many times, we men are too quick to "lower the boom" when we believe our child has violated the rules. Mothers are often more patient. They understand the limits of a young child's patience with frustration or their losing battle with exhaustion. They may empathize more easily with your child's fear and disappointment. A wise mother understands how all these can contribute to a child's "naughtiness." Fathers can learn these things, so don't be reluctant to watch your wife and learn from her.

2. <u>Learn from other men.</u>

Another bit of ancient common sense observes that "there's nothing new under the sun."[43] That certainly applies to being a good father. No matter what the challenge you face—finding time for your children while carrying a heavy work load, guiding a teen through adolescence, or caring for a newborn—there's at least one other father around you who has faced the same dilemma. Why get discouraged? Why try to "reinvent the wheel"? Why struggle to work it out alone? Go find another father, or group of fathers, and talk.

Mothers learned the value of this generations ago. Grandma or an aunt or two were usually nearby and ready to give advice and encouragement to new or struggling mothers. In pre-industrial days, mothers met at the public well or the stream where they washed clothes. Later, they'd meet and share tips and encouragement at church meetings or over coffee around the kitchen table. They learned from experience that, when parenting challenges and questions arise, two heads (or more) are better than one!

Why should mothers get all the advice and encouragement? Fathers need it, too. If you're struggling to balance your job and the needs of your family, have lunch with another man who seems to be doing well at that and ask him how he does it. If your teen is a particular challenge to you now, call up an older parent who's children are grown. Ask for his advice. You'll be surprised and encouraged by the help you receive. Then, be ready to share the same when someone else calls you!

101

3. Learn from your children.

Our children don't just learn from us, they teach us, also. So be willing to listen to them and learn.

"What is it that my children need from me, anyway?" one father asked me. "I know they need my love and financial support, but is there anything else?" My reply was simple. "Ask them. They'll tell you." I explained that I didn't mean he had to literally ask them. Just listening and observing carefully will often tell you what your child needs—and wants from you.

Teenagers especially need fathers who really listen to them. Walt Mueller, President of the Center for Parent/Youth Understanding tells the story of sixteen year-old Sarah who was suffering from a combination of anorexia and bulimia, both serious eating disorders.

Sarah came from an upper middle class family and was a "straight A" student. She doesn't know why she was sick but decided that it was probably because she thought "that if I really got sick people would pay attention to me. The irony of it is that my father is a psychologist," she said. Walt said that Sarah's problems were really "a loud cry for help that the most important man in her life never heard. Too busy with the demands of work and time spent listening to other people's problems, her father's deaf ears were forcing his little girl to fall deeper and deeper into the pit of adolescent despair. What she wanted and needed, more than anything else, was a dad who listened to her."[44]

A teen whose grades are dropping or whose behavior has changed suddenly may be crying out for his father's attention or for firm limits that show your love. Even young children quickly learn to get attention by "acting up." If your young child is always interrupting you to ask questions or to ask you to do something with them, maybe they're just curious or need to learn better manners. But maybe they need a few minutes of time to play or read a story and feel like the most important person in your world. Our children tell us what they need from us. Are you listening?

4. Learn from yourself.

Remember, you know your children better than anyone else. You've watched them, listened to them, loved them, and learned from them longer than anyone other than their mother. You know more than you may think you do. Remember: You are the best father your child could have.

So, trust your own common sense. Trust your judgement when it says, "Ask my wife," "Be patient and listen here," or "Check with a friend." God gave you to those children and no one else can be as good a father to them as you can be. When it comes to being their father, you're the "expert." Learn from yourself. Trust your judgement.

5. Learn from your Heavenly Father.

When Harry Chapin wrote a song about the father who lamented that his son had "grown up just like me," it was sad, but not surprising. Fathers have an enormous influence on their children. And much of how we "father" our children is learned from how our father "fathered" us.

That can be a problem, not only when a child is raised without a father (and has no model to learn from) but also when a father is alcoholic, abusive, emotionally absent, or authoritarian in style. And nobody's perfect, including the best fathers. They all passed on some unhealthy parenting practices or attitudes to us.

Where do we go to shed the imperfect ways we learned from our fathers? How do we re-learn fathering, or even (if we never knew our father) learn it for the first time? Go right to the top. Start with the best. There's no better place to go than to God, our Heavenly Father. He's the one and only perfect father.

How well do you know him? If you want to learn how to be a good father from him, you'll need to spend time getting to know him. As your relationship deepens, you'll find that the way he fathers you will shape and mold the way you father your children. Whether you need to learn fathering for the first time or re-learn it, your Heavenly Father can teach you to be the best father you can be.

As you experience God's daily love and care, you'll grow more loving and caring. As you appreciate his patience and forgiveness, you'll be able to be more patient and forgiving with your children. As you understand the wisdom of his loving limits, the balance of his kindness and firmness, you'll become a wiser, kinder and fairer father. As you come to see how, in Jesus Christ, God is humble and a servant, you'll be freed to be a loving, humble servant to your family, also.

Becoming more like your Heavenly Father not only makes you a better father but also a better man. In contrast to the vision of those who want masculinity and fatherhood to disappear into a basically feminized "parenthood," loving your wife and children with the love of God, "represents the fulfillment, the completeness of masculinity, and ultimately the transcendence of gender."[45] Learning from our Heavenly Father makes us more fully and completely men. Fatherhood and manhood are inseparable. Only men can be fathers, just as only women can be mothers. In his perfection, God embodies the highest of both masculinity and femininity. We men will always be men first, but the Father can help us begin to embody the best that all parents can be.

Let's say it in terms we used earlier: *Good Parenting Begins with Good Personing.* As you get to know God more deeply and let him make you a better man you'll become a much better father. To put it yet another way: *As You deepen your relationship with God, you'll become a better father.* It's inevitable. Guaranteed. It can't fail! God is the perfect father. As you get to know him better and better, you'll become convinced of that. If you want to be a better father, then, learn from the best. Learn from him. All highly successful fathers do that.

A Note to Single Fathers

Whether you're a father who's separated from your children by divorce or because you've never married their mother, you're still a father. Most of what I said in this chapter applies to you. You can be a highly successful parent, too.

Your children need you, and you have so much to give them. Remember what we said earlier in this chapter: research shows that dads do make a difference—even (and especially) divorced dads who stay actively involved in the lives of their children. So be their provider. Don't let them suffer the economic fate of so many children separated from their fathers. Be their protector, nurturer, and sponsor whenever and however you can.[46] Guide them, affirm them, encourage them, and train them to live successfully in the world.

And remember that you need your children. Studies show that, as you guide your children into adulthood and maintain a close and loving bond with them, you'll likely have a higher sense of self-esteem.[47] So as you struggle to be a good father to them, they'll give you much in return. It'll be worth all the effort!

If you need help or you just get discouraged, remember this: there are plenty of fathers just like you. Join with them. Learn from them. Listen to them. You may not be able to listen to your wife for parenting insights, but there are other mothers (perhaps even your own) who would be happy to help. Don't be afraid to ask. We married fathers want to help, also. I've never been a single father, but I do know many. I've seen the special challenges and obstacles they face in being fathers to their children. I've seen how hard it can be for them. But I've also seen how hard they work at being good fathers and how successful they can be. If we married fathers can help, please ask us.

Don't give up! You and your children need each other. As all highly successful fathers do, rely on your

Heavenly Father. Learn from him. Let other successful parents help you. **You** can be a highly successful parent. You're the best father your children could have. Just keep working to be the best person and father you can possibly be. Both you and your children will be grateful that you did.

Chapter 5

Rome Wasn't Built in a Day

When I was a young child, eager to learn to ride my bicycle perfectly the first time, I heard those words. As a high school student struggling to write a paper that took me longer than I hoped, I heard them. Someone said them to me when, as an adult working to build my career, I complained that it was developing more slowly than planned. "Rome wasn't built in a day."

As a child, I wondered just what that phrase meant. What did the capital of Italy have to do with me? But experience taught me that those words were meant both as wise counsel (against taking harmful short cuts and trying to finish something important too quickly) and good encouragement to keep on working until I reached my goal. Great achievements often require patient investments of time and energy. After all, the great city of Rome "wasn't built in a day."

Highly successful parents are convinced that being a successful parent and building a successful family takes time. It requires a patient "keeping on, keeping on" doing and being the best that you can. There aren't any shortcuts.

Unfortunately, time is something of which parents seem to have less and less today. As one parent put it, "The world has stepped on the gas and it seems there's no turning back."[1] We live in an "instant society" of microwaves, fast food, and fax machines. I've received faxes at my home in New York all the way from Australia, putting me in instant communication with friends on the other side of the world. And when dinner is running late, we've turned to the microwave or local fast food place more than once! In some ways, I'm grateful for our "instant society."

But what lesson does our "instant society" teach us? To give important efforts a significant investment of our time? To be patient and avoid short cuts? Hardly. The unspoken, but clear message of the instant society is just the opposite; that great rewards can be gained with little effort; that significant, lasting, and rewarding relationships, such as those in families, can be built overnight.[2]

Highly successful parents know better. When time pressures begin to chip away at their investment in their family relationships, they remember that, just as "Rome wasn't built in a day," strong, successful families aren't, either.

Time is of the Essence

Children enrich our lives in ways we can't even imagine before they are given to us. But parenting them is surely a time-intensive task! Children don't just ask for our time—they grab it in large doses, daily. They fit uncomfortably in our instant society; unwelcome intruders in our time starved world. Like beggars in the subway, they remind us of urgent needs and obligations. And often, they make us feel guilty.

"Time is of the essence," we say. But as one astute observer has said, when it comes to successful parenting, time *is* the essence. "Love is the foundation for the family," and "time is the medium for [that] love."[3] Through the giving of this most precious commodity—our time—our children experience the concrete reality of our love for them.

Time together is the soil within which family relationships grow and are nurtured. It is the glue that holds families— especially busy families—together. "Time is money" is another common maxim. It also reminds us how precious our time is. Highly successful parents might say it slightly differently, however. They know that to a young child, time with their parents is more than money. It's love.

Child Psychologist Dr. Penelope Leach reminds us that young children aren't mind readers. They can't guess at love. They need to see and feel regular expressions of their parents' love for them. Those of us who have or have had toddlers and preschoolers know that it seems they always need just a little more of our time and attention than we can give them! Nonetheless, she says, "If they are to be sure that love is not a one-way street, the times when you ignore them or shrug them off need to be balanced by times when you seek their company and ask them for a conversation or game."[4]

Giving them those few moments whenever you can, by really listening to them and really sharing their world for a few moments, conveys the message that they, and their thoughts, really are important to you. And it also builds bridges of communication that you'll be very thankful for when the teenage years arrive!

Highly successful parents understand that time together "heads children's list of most precious parental gifts."[5] Of all the ways they can be generous with their children, these parents know that giving them their time and attention is the most special of all.[6]

Some years ago, actress Sally Field received an Oscar for her performance in the movie "Norma Rae." At the ceremony, during her acceptance speech, she held up the statuette and said, smiling broadly, "You like me! You really like me!" That's what receiving that award said to her. That's the message our children receive when we share time together with them. Taking your daughter on a business trip, including your son in your hobby, putting aside your work to play a short game; all these say to your children. "You're important to me. I enjoy you. I like being with you." What an incredible gift to your child's self-esteem!

Really Being There

Pam, age forty, is a photographer and her husband, Doug, age forty-two, is a free lance journalist. They both have busy and demanding careers. They also have a seven year-old son and a three year-old daughter. Obviously, they didn't rush into parenthood while very young, but still, the demands of parenting surprised them.

"When we decided to have children, we thought we could be those happy, working parents," Pam said. But soon they discovered that meeting the demands of career and parenthood, though quite possible, is rarely easy. "For a long time," Pam admitted, "even when we were home, we were overwhelmed by the emotional commitment our kids needed. We kept thinking that if we didn't think about it, it would go away."[7] But of course, it didn't. It took them some time to realize that their children needed more of their time and emotional energy. And when they realized it, they were threatened by it at first. But gradually, Pam and Doug came to accept their children's emotional needs and provide for them.

Highly successful parents not only recognize that their children require their time and emotional commitments , but they find ways to meet them—at least most of the time. Like many parents, Pam and Doug learned "on the job" as their children grew. And they used what they learned to make necessary changes so they could be more emotionally available to their children. Pam, particularly, made some changes.

She began to see the need for some changes when a neighbor observed that their son, Peter, looked depressed. "I suddenly saw him at 14," Pam said. "I had this vision of

110

someone offering him some drugs." She said she envisioned him in a drug rehabilitation program or even dead. That's when she decided to go back to working free lance so she'd have more time to be with her son and daughter. It would be hard to manage, she knew, but "I can't tell you how much happier I've been ever since." Chances are that Peter and his sister are happier, too![8]

It wasn't as easy for a friend of mine. "Mommy, you're answering, but you're not really listening to me." My friend's 5 year-old daughter heard her mother's mumbled replies, saw her mother's wandering eyes and knew that her mother wasn't really listening to her.

That's another pitfall we busy parents face when we try to meet our children's need for our time and availability-being **there** with our children but not really **being** there. Our body is there, but our mind is focused on the current project at work, the sports show on TV, or a pressing household chore. Sooner or later, our children realize what's happening.

So when you can give your child a few moments, make them count. Give your undivided attention. Be available to "go with the flow" of your child's conversation, wherever it leads. Listen for their input and try to really make a connection with your child's life and feelings. This connection gradually forms the ties that bind parents and children together and, paradoxically, frees them to know the great joy that comes from being bound up together in the great bundle of life we call "family." Which of us wants to be too busy for that?

"Five Minute Possibilities"

I know some parents who resolved that they would, indeed, spend some significant amounts of time really enjoying their children. But when? Most of the week, life was just too hectic. The time and energy just wasn't there.

Since they were not able to really be involved with their children's lives during the week, they decided to make it up on the weekend. Every weekend was scheduled with family outings, meals together, and lots of planned fun.

How did it work out? Not badly, but it wasn't entirely satisfying for either the parents or children. They did have some very pleasant times together. But after a few weekends, things began to change. If a friend invited them for a birthday party or overnight, the children would resent the family's weekend plans. Soon, the parents and children began to dread the weekend as just an extension of the busy, overscheduled work week. Both became increasingly unhappy. What was the problem?

As I discussed in my book, *It's the Little Things that Count,*[9] weekends are an important time for families to have fun together and nurture healthy relationships. But such an "all or nothing" approach to family time as my friends tried isn't healthy! And it really isn't hard to understand why.

I suspect that most of us eat pretty regularly; three meals daily at certain "standard" times of the day. Few of us would want to go on a "feast or famine" regimen where we eat all our food heavily and continuously for a few days and then eat nothing at all for the next few days. That's not healthy. Our bodies need regular, daily amounts of nutritious food in order to remain healthy. That's the way it is with our children's need for our time and attention, also.

Author Paul Lewis astutely points out a pitfall especially common to fathers. We dads often think of family time as the big, expensive and extravagant "events" rather than small, often spontaneous ones. "Children, however," he observes, "are far more affected by the consistency of regular, smaller moments."[10] In order to be emotionally healthy, children need regular "doses" of our time and attention . These doses can be small (just 5 or 10 minutes) but they need to be administered regularly, usually daily, in order to promote good emotional health.

Preschool and younger elementary age children have a wonderful ability to live in the "now." Their sense of time and the future is still developing. Waiting even a week for their birthday or Christmas seems like forever to a young child. It's so hard to wait!

Young children live on their own schedules. Just ask any parent who's trying to explain to their hungry preschooler that dinner is coming in just an hour! I know a mother who jokingly called the hour before dinner the "Arsenic Hour" because the children got so hungry and irritable, she was tempted to feed them arsenic! The "adult" meal schedule doesn't quite fit young children sometimes. They have their own schedules when it comes to eating.

Emotional "Feeding"

It's the same way with the emotional "feeding" that comes from a few minutes with Mom or Dad. Children need regular meals! And their "meal times" don't always fit our crowded schedules. Waiting is hard. And waiting four or five days to tell Mom or Dad about their new friend at day care or to read a special book or play a game together is almost impossible!

Lewis challenges fathers to look for regular, daily "five minute fathering possibilities" such as telling your children about one of your childhood mistakes, listening to one of your child's favorite songs, offering a foot or back rub (and seeing what conversation may result) or even wearing yourself out with five minutes of wrestling or horsy rides![11]

That's good advice for both parents. As busy and tired as we often are, we can still look for brief but regular "five minute parenting possibilities" that provide those small, daily doses of time and attention which our children need from us. They're available within every family's schedule each day.

So rather than trying to fit most of your time with your children into a few big blocks, mostly on weekends, look for a few minutes once or twice every day to connect with your child. For example, when you're preparing dinner, let your child help (in an appropriate way that really does help) such as putting out napkins or placemats. After dinner when you sit to pay bills or read correspondence, invite your child to do homework at the table with you. Surprisingly, that can be good time spent together. One 10 year-old boy said, "When Mom helps me with my homework is our best time because she spends time alone with me, and I understand it better!"[12]

Or invite your child to sit nearby and draw a picture for the letter you're writing to Grandma. You can even watch videos 15 minutes at a time. A 10 or 15 minute board game, a few minutes working together on a family project, discussing "one good thing and one bad thing that happened today" over dinner, even doing homework—these are just some of the "little things" that don't take much time, but like daily vitamins, they help grow emotionally healthy children and strong family relationships. The point is to provide opportunities for you and your children to be together and share in the business of being a family after being apart all day.[13] Then, any weekend fun will be a bonus!

If you're a single parent who generally only sees your child on a weekend, the temptation is to plan a "big time" every time. And sometimes, that's just great. But other times, the best time you can share with your child is found in the regular business of your life (projects and chores) or theirs (soccer games or homework). And why not see if you can spend one evening during the week helping your child with homework or taking her to band practice? These times don't seem very special, but they're the stuff of normal family life that our children do enjoy sharing with us.

Bedtime—Not Just for Little Ones

Sharing bedtime with our children is one of those special emotional "vitamins" that should be taken daily, if possible. For younger children, it offers a ritual that, by its very sameness and also its pleasure, assures them of your continuing love and care for them. A little fun ritual makes bedtime special, and doesn't have to take very long.

When our children were preschoolers, my wife would tell them brief made up stories about three fictional characters she invented: Hankey, Blankey and Boo-Boo. They always did crazy things (some of which clearly resembled things my wife did as a child) and had a lot of fun in the process. For a few years, these stories were a very popular part of the bedtime ritual at our house. With a prayer and bible story, bedtime offers the opportunity for a daily affirmation of God's love and care for your children and the entire family, too.

But bedtime isn't just a special time for younger children. When my oldest son was in high school, he often would come up to our room at bedtime (ours, not his—we usually were asleep long before he was!) He might have been taking a break from homework or be returning from an evening activity. He'd flop down on the bed and talk; sometimes about his day, sometimes about a future plan or decision, and sometimes about just anything. It was clear that he just wanted to "be there" and "connect."

My wife and I quickly learned to put down our reading and listen during those visits. If this was when he wanted to talk, we wanted him to know we were happy to listen! These conversations usually weren't long (maybe three or four minutes), but they did keep us in touch and were often happily surprising.

I learned something valuable from that experience. Now, I go in and say good night to my younger son, whether he asks or not. Sure, it's a little thing, but who knows what conversation will develop as a result? So don't neglect bedtime in your search for those small, daily doses of time with your children. Bedtime is there every day, it doesn't take long, and it's not just for young children, either.

Just Around The Corner

Paul Lewis writes particularly for fathers, but his advice applies to both Moms and Dads, especially those in two career families where both parents have demanding jobs. One of the biggest obstacles we face in sharing time with our children is what Lewis calls the "Around the Corner" syndrome!

These are extremely competitive economic times. Both men and women are concerned with maintaining and getting ahead in their careers. This sets parents up to fall into the "Around the Corner" trap. Lewis says:

> You think if you put in extra hours for the next six months, the result will be a nice raise or big commission, a payoff from a substantial project completed or maybe a new business over the hump and on its way. Of course, the cost will be weeks and maybe months of extra long hours.[14]

With an important end in view, however, we expect our spouse and children to accept that cost and understand that we just can't be available as much as we'd like, at least temporarily. But, it'll all be worth it in the end. "Just as soon as you turn this corner, your schedule will relax and the resources will be there to enjoy new freedoms and the benefits of all this hard work."[15]

The danger, Lewis points out, is that while we're waiting to turn the corner, we may miss whole chunks of our children's childhood. We just won't be there for both the special times and the everyday moments that fill the hearts

116

and memories of parents (and children) long after their children are grown.

Thinking only of how great things would be "just around the corner," it's hard to see that "invariably, around the corner is another corner to get around. Something beyond your control didn't work out right and so the grand payoff doesn't come."[16] After years of getting around corner after corner, suddenly, it's too late. You realize you really don't know your older children or don't like what they've become as they've grown up.

The Tables Turn

The late Harry Chapin captured the pain of that realization in his song "Cat's in The Cradle." It tells of a father who was away from home most of the time when his son was young because "there were planes to catch and bills to pay. He learned to walk while I was away." But his son idolized his father and, in the song's refrain, says over and over, "I'm gonna be like you, Dad. You know I'm gonna be like you."

When, as a ten year-old, the boy asks his dad to play catch, his dad says he's too busy. "When you comin' home, Dad?" "I don't know when," his dad replied, "but we'll be together then. You know we'll have a good time then." All the while, the boy smiled and said "I'm gonna be like him, yeah. You know I'm gonna be like him."

Chapin's song goes on to tell how the dad wanted to talk to his son during one of his visits home from college. "Son, I'm proud of you, Can you sit for awhile?" The father shouldn't have been surprised at his son's reply. "What I'd really like, Dad, is to borrow the car keys. See you later. Can I have them, please?"

The last verse of the song is surely the saddest. It tells how the father tries to connect with his son after retirement. But by then, it's too late. Here's how Chapin poignantly describes that episode:

> I've long since retired, my son's moved away.
> I called him up just the other day.
> I said, 'I'd like to see you if you don't mind.'
> He said. 'I'd love to, Dad, if I can find the time.
> You see, my job's a hassle and the kids have the flu,
> but it's sure nice talkin' to you, Dad.
> It's been sure nice talkin' to you.'
> And as I hung up the phone it occurred to me,
> He'd grown up just like me.
> My boy was just like me.[17]

Another dad was determined that his story would turn out differently. He recalled the pain he felt as a ten year-old boy when his dad was so busy that he never seemed to have time for him. He vowed to be different with his own children.

> I said to myself...that if I ever had children of my own, I would give them a great deal of support— spiritual or whatever they needed—and I would be with them. I can vividly remember the day my dad died. I came home from the hospital and there was a picture of both my parents on the bureau. I went up to the picture and I looked up at my dad and said "Dad, it's shame I never knew you." I made a vow to myself that this would never occur in my family and I do spend time with the kids.[18]

Highly successful fathers (and mothers, too) live by the conviction that good parenting takes time. So they commit themselves to taking, and making, the time and attention their children need in small, regular doses. They've learned to make the most of the daily experiences of family life, bedtime, homework, mealtime, chores and many others, in order to share time with their children. These parents use the many five-minute parenting possibilities available every day. They know that successfully parenting their children takes time and, even though they're very busy, they know there are lots of practical ways to provide it.

How Much "Quality" in "Quality Time"?

For the past two decades, many busy parents have relied on the concept of "quality time" to meet the emotional needs of their children and to help relieve the guilt and anxiety they feel when they can't give their children all the time they want to.

"Quality time" is an idea first generated in the '70's. As more and more mothers entered the workforce and spent large parts of their day away from their young children, parents searched for some way to compensate for the lost time with their children. Child development specialists who studied children in day care pointed out that short, active interactions between care-givers and children were far superior to long periods of passive care. In short, they said, it wasn't the *quantity* of time parents spent with their children that really mattered, but the *quality* of that time. Even though this quality time might be brief, it could still be full of intense, high caliber parent-child interactions. Scheduled whenever the family could manage to be together, it would make up for the all the long absences in-between.[19]

Over the years, however, parents have discovered that there are some very real problems with the idea of quality time. Guided by their common sense and parenting instincts, highly successful parents are beginning to "question the very concept of quality time." They suspect that "it's too easy to use this as an excuse not to spend time with children on a regular basis."[20]

If quality time means that "you must cram in a day's worth of activities between sunset and bedtime," it's no help at all![21] It only produces guilt and frustration—two qualities of which most busy parents already have plenty! After a long day at work (or day care), most parents and children don't have the energy for a big production in the evening.

Successful parents also "part company with the experts on the notion of quality superseding quantity." They understand that you can't have one without the other. Like so many of life's gifts, real quality time with those we love can't always be produced on demand. We can only make the space in our lives and create the conditions within which quality time can happen. "The more time spent with or near a child—be it playing a game, drying dishes or reading quietly in the same room—the more quality time is likely to occur."[22]

With all this in mind, many families have arrived at the conclusion that the notion of quality time is plainly "absurd."[23] One parent, when asked about it, said bluntly "Forget about quality time. Just be there."[24] I don't believe it's necessary to throw out the idea of quality time altogether, but it certainly needs to be re-defined if it's going to be helpful to both parents and their children. So let's look at what a useful understanding of quality time is and isn't.

Busier is Not Always Better

First, and most importantly, quality time with our children isn't constantly entertaining them or scheduling an uninterrupted avalanche of fun, activity, and conversation with them. That's neither practical nor healthy. There is a place for those special and "big" events, like a trip to the amusement park or museum. But they're special precisely because they are occasional and, therefore, so different from the many smaller, quieter, regular activities that make up the normal flow of family life.

We've all got plenty to do when we're at home evenings and weekends. Few of us can focus all our attention on our child each evening after work. But, as Dr. Penelope Leach points out, once past infancy, our children don't want our time just for "play," they want to share in our lives. And that means sharing in our regular activities. "Real" quality time, she says, may not be a special game or story, but going with Dad to do something as personal as changing clothes or as mundane as getting the car washed. The child receives the magic message: "I want your company."[25]

Parents have "homework" many evenings, too! Working nearby, perhaps at the same table or in the same room, allows your child to feel a sense of "togetherness" with you whether they help you with a chore or do their own activity while you write bills. And you can share a conversation at the same time. During these few moments, your children share in the natural rhythm of family life with you. But when your every moment together is highly scheduled, such sharing isn't possible. Yet, that is exactly what makes family life rewarding and worthwhile for you both.[26]

Some evenings and weekends, brief, quiet, low stress activities will be just what everyone needs. Playing a game together for just 10-15 minutes after dinner, taking a walk or bike ride through the neighborhood, reading a short story or chapter of a favorite book all can be renewing oases of quality time at the end of a long day. But don't feel you have to be doing something together every minute. Parents and children alike need some "alone time" to be quiet and recharge their emotional batteries for the new day ahead.

One of the most vivid memories my oldest son has from his elementary school days is the weekend he and I flew out of town on a business trip together. We had time to talk and be together during the plane rides and, for a few hours that weekend, he felt very grown-up and a part of my life. I was busy during most of the weekend, but we did have a good time together. Quality time isn't always just fun and games.

Not Always Educational

Second, quality time isn't necessarily "educational" time. You probably know parents whose idea of quality time with their children is to teach them how to fish or cook or build a model car or work a computer. Maybe you had a parent like that!

As a father, I know how easy it is to change a relaxed game of catch into a instructional session on playing the outfield! All of a sudden, the tone of our fun time takes on a hard edge. "No, that's not right. Do it this way." "You'll never be any good at baseball until you learn to catch the ball properly."

There's certainly a time for this kind of teaching, but if you're hoping to share some quality time with your child, both of you have to want to do the activity in question, and both of you ought to be enjoying yourselves! Don't just assume that your child shares your interests. The point of quality time is to share theirs! What do they like to do that you can both enjoy doing together?

Third, quality time isn't always initiated by parents. If we're tuned in to our children, they'll often let us know what they'd like to do with us. Sometimes, it's enough to say, "I've got a few minutes right now. I'd enjoy doing something with you. Is there anything you'd like to do?" With preschool children, you can say "Would you like to play (name a favorite game) or do something else?" Let your children lead you. That's much of the excitement of time together for them; you get into their world on their terms.

And sometimes, while you're "just being around" without any agenda, or doing a chore nearby where your child is playing, a conversation will just happen. You may not have been actively trying to start one, but you were there and you were available—and it happened. But if you're never "just around," those conversations can't "just happen."

One parent describes how this worked with her teenagers. Their family schedules were pretty full. There wasn't a lot of time for "frequent family adventures." And, as parents of teenagers know, teens rarely like to hang out with the "old folks" anyway! So for this parent, quality time with her teen included a "passive presence, a willingness to make ourselves available for support, if and when the kids need us or are ready to talk." And she was right about one thing: "when the kids want to talk, they want to talk now, even if it is to us parent-types, even if it's because we're the only ones around."[27] So it's vital that we be around!

Highly successful parents know that while quality time isn't always initiated by parents, sometimes it should be. Even though young children always seem to want more time and attention than their parents can give, "the times when you ignore or shrug them off need to be balanced by times when you seek their company and ask them for a conversation or game."[28] It's during those times that quality time happens, too!

"Blue Sky Time"

Successful parents won't give up the idea of quality time altogether, but they understand the need to "create a little slack"[29] so that the time they share with their children really can be a relaxed, enjoyable time for all. With that in mind, let's start our re-definition of "quality time" this way: *Quality time with our children includes not only those occasional big, fun and expensive activities, but also plenty of what one observer called "blue sky time"*—the unstructured, "hangin' out" time when we're together or nearby and available to our children.

Driving to the store or in the carpool, working together in the yard, or reading and doing homework in the same room provide that "passive presence" that the parent of a teenager referred to. We could just as accurately call it "hangin' out" together. Ellen Galinsky, Co-Founder of the Families and Work Institute in New York City, says that it is during this "loose, unstructured time that kids often bring up feelings that don't surface on demand, the 'little pains of the day.'" She also notes that "it's through sharing them that real parent-child closeness" develops.[30]

We saw that illustrated in our own family many times. My wife and I made it a priority for one of us to be there as often as possible when our sons came home from school. By the time they reached adolescence, if we asked them how the day was or what happened, we'd often get one of two unenlightening answers—either "Fine" or "Ugh."

Of course, as soon as they'd run in the door, they'd head directly to the refrigerator. But we discovered that if we hung around until that feeding frenzy was satisfied, they'd often start to talk about their day. All of a sudden, I'd find myself in a conversation that actually did contain entire sentences and revealing thoughts!

It's true, as one parent noted, that the best way to get your child to talk about him or her self is not just to ask questions. Adolescents hate questions. They consider you nosey. A better approach is to "share something from your own day with your child...that gives your child a chance to chime in and share a silly, sad or angry moment from [their] day, too."[31]

When our youngest son entered adolescence, I began to appreciate the brief (and it was usually only ten brief minutes or so) just-home-from-school time more and more. As children get older, they often become more private and it takes them longer to get their feelings out. So that unstructured, "blue sky" time when you're available just in case they want to talk is even more important. And, as one parent put it, "if we don't try to make that time available now and then, we'll miss many special moments, the 'chocolate truffles' of having children."[32]

Not all of us can be there after school, of course. But after school is one of many opportunities. As we've already seen, there are other times built into the fabric of family life (mealtime, bedtime, chores, homework, etc.) that are just as special.

Kill Two Birds

In addition to "blue sky" time, then, *quality time is usually found right in the middle of normal, everyday family routines.* Busy parents don't have to pile on guilt because they can't spend three hours every night after work doing something special and wonderful with their children. There are some real opportunities for quality time built right into the routines of daily family life.

"Eating dinner together, even when the food is take-out, counts for a lot."[33] That's when busy families gather, if only briefly, to remind themselves that they're more than just people living under the same roof. They are a family; people that God has given to each other to share together in the great adventure of life.

If your children are elementary school age, you don't have to worry about long, drawn out quality time at meals. They probably want to eat quickly and get right back to playing with their friends! But just those 10 or 15 minutes together every day can be surprisingly rewarding. For example, try asking everyone to tell one good thing and one bad thing that happened at work or school that day (parents go first!). And hold hands as you say your prayer of thanks for the food.

As we've seen, bedtime can be a very special daily quality time, especially for toddlers and preschoolers. They love a bedtime story or quiet game. And you can talk or sing a favorite song or say a nursery rhyme together during bath-time, too. Someone even suggested setting up a mobile over your child's changing table or some colorful stick-ups on the wall nearby so that you can have a fun talk with your toddler during diaper changes! Now that's what I call creative![34] It is also wonderful stimulation for their young mind.

Of course, we all face the inevitable times when we can't be there for our child's bedtime, however much we want to be. When those times unavoidably start piling up, turn to the telephone. If you're away from home on a business trip, call home at bedtime to say goodnight to your child or say prayers with them. Or call home on an afternoon break or at dinner time to let them know you're still "connected." The message is clear: "I'm not there, but I'm still thinking of you. I'm available. I care."

Many daily family routines are often brief, inexpensive, and even mundane. Yet they provide the stuff of many rewarding "quality times." How? By holding within themselves the potential for allowing you and your child to share together in the great adventure of life; helping, supporting, teaching, enjoying, and, most of all, loving each other. That's what makes any time really quality time.

Striking A Balance

So, "Rome wasn't built in a day." Highly successful parenting is a time intensive activity, too. There's no other way to do it. Of course, even the most successful parents can't spend all the time they want with their children. They can't always drop everything and focus everything on a child. And it doesn't do any good to feel guilty! The key is to find a healthy balance between the needs of your children and all the other demands on your time. And even finding the right balance takes some experimenting, some trial, and some error. It also takes time.

But when the balance is struck and we give ourselves to our children, even for those special, brief moments, "we are sending them a love message more plainly than anything we could say. It's a love message we may forget, but they rarely will."[35] And successful parents know that it does pay off in the end. Common sense tells us that "You get back what you put in," and that applies to parenting, too.

But in the midst of busy lives, highly successful parents live by the conviction that good parenting can't be hurried. They struggle and pray and ask God's guidance to set their priorities and then make the necessary adjustments in their schedules. That way they don't waste time feeling guilty! They're creative, committed, and they take the time (and make the time) to nurture and enjoy their children. Of course, it's work and a constant struggle, but they know that accomplishing anything worthwhile takes time and effort. And they're convinced that, in the long run, every sacrifice will be well worth it. They'll get back what they put in—and much, much more.

Chapter 6

Live by the Golden Rule

"All you need is love" to solve any problem, pop songs tell us. If things aren't going right, just "put a little love in your heart." Isn't it true? Isn't love a parent's best guide for raising their children? Yes, of course. But most of us need a practical guide to help us put our love for our children into action in daily family life. Highly successful parents rely on the "Golden Rule."

"Do to others as you would have them do to you," Jesus said.[1] Though it's been ridiculed and caricatured ("The one who has the gold rules," or, "Do unto others, but be sure you do them first!"), it's widely accepted both as sound teaching, and good, common sense. *Highly successful parents are convinced that the Golden Rule remains the best guide to success in all human relationships, including parenting.*

Does that sound surprising? Do we really need the Golden Rule for successful parenting? If we already love our children, what practical effect on our parenting can it possibly have? Let me put it to you this way: Besides love, what is it that adults want most from others? My guess would be respect. Respect is love in action. Knowing we are respected as valuable individuals enables us to feel self-respect and a greater measure of happiness.

Children, too, want and need to feel respected. When they feel respected as individuals with their own value, interests, opinions, and feelings, they can feel really loved. When they feel respected, they can develop the self-respect they need to become happy, productive, and responsible adults. But children don't just want or need our respect, they deserve it, too. "Do unto others," Jesus said. Children are certainly "others." More than that, Jesus held them up to his followers as a spiritual example.[2] He made it clear that children deserve our respect!

Golden Rule of Parenting

The old common sense maxim says, "You can lead a horse to water but you can't force it to drink." We can teach and demonstrate for our children how to live responsibly and happily. We can share our values and faith with them daily. We can't, however, force them to adopt our values and faith. Ultimately, they will choose for themselves.

Children who feel loved and respected are more likely to want to please their parents and model after them in faith and values. Parents who practice the Golden Rule foster *mutual* respect in their families. They respect their children and expect the same in return. That encourages their children to drink deeply from the water of wise living to which they've been led. In the end, this mutual respect will be a big factor determining whether or not our children decide to follow in our footsteps as they walk through life. Dr. James Dobson notes that his own children grew up in an atmosphere of mutual respect. "That two sided coin," he says, is undoubtedly supported by biblical teaching and is a necessary and valuable part of successful parenting.[3]

So highly, successful parents apply their own version of the Golden Rule to everyday family life: *"I will treat my children with respect at all times and expect the same from them.* " But just how do you practice mutual respect in your home?

Teach it, Give it

Have you ever cringed as your young child repeated your words to a playmate in the very same way you first spoke them to him? I have, and it wasn't a pleasant experience! Children are great imitators. They learn to treat others the way they are treated and the way they see others in their family treated.

The best way to develop mutual respect in your family is for you and your spouse to practice it. Show your mutual respect by how you speak and listen to each other; by the way you serve each other in both the big and little things of daily life. Even toddlers and preschoolers (the greatest imitators!) can see what respect looks like. Then, they can begin to practice it!

As you give that same respect to your children, "this respect quickly becomes mutual. When you base decisions about managing your child's behavior on your understanding of his interests, preferences, needs and concerns, he begins to sense the care and regard that you have for him. As a result, he develops the same kind of respect for you and wants to behave in ways that please you."[4] As we'll see, this has some important implications for our approach to discipline. But now, let's look at some other practical ways to respect our children.

The Five Minute Warning

When our oldest son was in preschool, I learned my first lesson in treating him with respect. When I would tell him it was time to stop playing and to put his coat on so we could leave, he'd often whine about "not being done yet" and continue playing. At first, I assumed it was just stubbornness (from his mother's side of the family, of course!). Then, a more experienced parent advised me, "Why not give him a few minutes notice of the need to leave whenever possible. That way, he can wind up his playing and adjust to your schedule."

So the "five minute warning" (often followed by a "two minute warning") became one of my regular parenting tools—and it worked! It also made sense. No one likes to be torn away from something they enjoy, at least without a few minutes to come to a comfortable place to stop. Children are the same way. I learned to respect that in my children and avoided a lot of struggles as a result.

We've all seen the parents out at the mall or the grocery store with a young child at 9:00 p.m. at night. What's the child usually doing? Crying, screaming, or irritating his parents—maybe all three at once! What's the parent usually doing? Screaming, dragging, or spanking the child—maybe all three at once!

Sometimes, circumstances conspire so that even sensitive, successful parents can't avoid such an unpleasant situation. But sometimes, it's just that they didn't think about their child being so tired that they lose what little self-control they've learned. If we're out with a young child at mealtime, hunger can cause the same problem. *Being respectful of the child means recognizing where the problem lies*, in **our** needs and schedule, not primarily with the child. Whenever possible, respectful parents avoid those situations or tend to the needs of their children first (feeding them just before leaving home, or seeing that they get a longer afternoon nap, for example).

Lessons from the Workplace

Since so many parents spend so much of their lives in the workplace, experiences there can also help us better understand how to respect our children. One mother, who worked outside the home, knew she would have to change how she spoke to her children. She had a habit of barking out orders to them like a drill sergeant in the Army. Now, she says she tries to ask nicely, at least the first time. Before opening her mouth, she may ask herself, "How would I talk to a co-worker about this?" That helps her be kinder and use a more respectful tone of voice with her children.[5]

A family therapist agrees with this mother's wise approach; "You'll get better results if you invite change rather than demand it."[6] Nobody likes being spoken to sharply or ordered around all the time. She recommends that, whenever possible, parents "put the sound of music in your voice. Avoid words like 'always' and 'never'. Lace your requests with 'Please' and 'Thank you.' It not only teaches respect, but good manners, too! "[7]

Have you ever been criticized harshly by your boss in front of your co-workers? If so, I suspect it was an embarrassing, very unpleasant experience. Your boss showed little respect for your dignity and feelings. Children feel the same way in similar situations. So when serious correction is necessary, it's loving and respectful to do it privately, whenever possible. One mother, who has three children, ages eight, six and four, has a unique way to spare her children the embarrassment of public correction. Whenever they are engaging in unacceptable behavior in public, she uses a code word (which each of the children has developed) to remind them.[8]

Again, Dr. James Dobson has a helpful insight; "Parents cannot expect their children to treat them with dignity if they do not do the same to begin with. Be gentle with your children's egos." We should also avoid embarrassing them in front of friends. "If possible, discipline should not be administered in public....Self-esteem is the most fragile attribute in human nature, and once damaged, it is nearly impossible to repair."[9] Correcting our children with respect just makes sense. After all, the point of the exercise is not to humiliate them but to teach them how to live! Private correction spares their tender feelings and fragile self-respect.

Highly successful parents understand how words can either build up or tear down a child's self-respect. They observe the Golden Rule in their conversation with their children. They refuse to belittle their children or let others do it. They avoid using sarcasm with their children—the potential damage is just too high.

So successful parents understand, in order to receive respect (from their children or anyone), they must first give it. "A sarcastic father who is biting in his criticism of his children cannot expect to receive their genuine respect in return. They might fear him enough to conceal their contempt, but they will often seek revenge in adolescence." He may be able to intimidate them for awhile, but if he does not treat them respectfully, "the children may return his hostility when they reach the safety of early adulthood."[10]

Respecting Privacy

Privacy has to do with control of our own space. That's why it's so important to adults that others respect their privacy. In different ways at different ages, privacy is important to children, too. Parenting by the Golden Rule means respecting the privacy of children.

One mother told of her six year-old daughter who, modeling after her mother, would say, "I want some privacy now," when she didn't want to be disturbed.[11] Sometimes, it's just motivated by a desire to play quietly without interruption or to take a break from continual interaction with others (just as adults wish for!).

Author Anne Cassidy, in her article *Rites of Privacy* describes how even younger children may desire privacy. A child in toilet training may hide a dirty diaper because they don't want to "broadcast" their accident. That's a request for privacy. Cassidy advises just removing the diaper without a fuss, assuring them they'll learn to do better, and dropping the subject.[12]

Any time after the age of five, children may develop a concern for physical modesty. That, too, is a desire for privacy which should be honored by parents as much as possible. Knocking on the bedroom and bathroom door before entering is a sign of respect for the privacy of a child (and teaches them to respect yours in the same way!). In fact, knocking before entering is a good practice to begin by the time a child is three or four years old.

Cassidy points out that the desire for privacy peaks during the teen years. Even innocent questions about school or friends can be interpreted as "prying" by privacy obsessed teens! So, ask questions sparingly, gently, and caringly—not suspiciously, she advises.

Teens, like all of us, build their self-respect on the foundation of their parents' respect. That's why it's critical for parents to respect their privacy as much as possible. One set of parents needed a receipt that their sixteen year-old son had left in his bedroom. They looked for it on top of his desk, but stopped short of digging through his drawers. "We just didn't feel comfortable rummaging through his things," his mother said. "I feel that it's our children's right to have a little space to themselves; a place where they know we won't go."[13]

Of course, it's not always so easy to respect the privacy of a teen. There's so much more they can be "up to" and so much dangerous behavior they can engage in. Respect for privacy is ultimately built on trust. "Unless parents believe in their child's ability to handle time alone in a responsible manner, they'll be reluctant" to respect their privacy. So highly successful parents aim to build a relationship of mutual respect and trust with their children that's well in place when the teen years arrive. Still, even the most respectful, successful parents act decisively in cases of danger to their children, such as alcohol, drugs or sexual activity. If parents have proof that their teen is "doing something harmful to herself or to another, there's nothing wrong with temporarily suspending some privacy rights" until the situation is resolved. Then, respect for privacy can be restored. [14]

Expect Respect

Highly successful parents know that respect is meant to be a two way street. So they not only give it to their children, they expect it in return.

We can all remember how, as children, we were expected to speak only when spoken to, be unfailingly polite, and never raise our voices to adults. That was the way we were to show them respect. At least those were the rules!

The rules have changed somewhat today. Many parents encourage their children to speak up when they have something to say. They don't allow shouting or whiny, argumentative "back talk" because it breeds mutual *disrespect*. But they do permit, and sometimes even encourage, children to respectfully state their opinions, even when they disagree. These parents understand that respect means really listening to their children (though it doesn't necessarily mean approval of everything they say!).

However you feel about that, most families still have some basic rules that help children learn to show respect for their parents. "Please be on time for meals" is one such rule. Being late for meals is disrespectful to the parent (or parents) who prepared it as well as the others who are there and ready to eat. "Clean up your messes" is another common one (This applies to children old enough to clean up without making a bigger mess!). Leaving it for a parent or sibling to clean up is disrespectful of them. And an important way children develop self-respect is by taking responsibility for their actions and cleaning up their messes.

"Please don't speak to me that way" or "Do I speak to you that way?" reminds children that parents, too, have feelings that can be hurt by harsh words. Their feelings need to be respected and protected, too. Even young children sense that the way we speak to each other reflects respect or a lack of it. So when your six year-old shouts "I hate you" or your teen angrily shouts that "You're an awful mother! You're not fair!" it's time to remind them that respect goes two ways. "I'm sorry you're angry, and I understand why, but I have too much respect for myself to let you talk to me that way. When you're under control, we can talk some more."

There'll always be some name calling and teasing between siblings and it's always subject to the *"DSSS Rule"* ("Don't Sweat The Small Stuff"). If, however, it goes beyond occasional "small stuff" to become a regular part of family life, it can quickly undermine mutual respect among siblings. Children who are subject to constant ridicule may also lose respect for their parents for not protecting them from it.

That's why parents who live by the Golden Rule want family conversation to reflect this wise advice: "Do not let any unwholesome talk come out of your mouths, but only what is helpful for building others up according to their needs, that it may benefit those who listen."[15] Nobody benefits from name calling, teasing and "put downs."

Dr. Ray Guarendi, a clinical psychologist, went right to the experts on family rules—one hundred and fifty healthy, successful families from all over the country. He asked the parents what rules they adopted. Here are some of the major ones they shared with him, as reported in his book, *Back to The Family.*[16]

- No back-talk, name calling, or put-downs
- No foul language
- "Please" and "Thank you" are required
- Wait to talk until others are finished
- No borrowing without asking first

- If you buy candy, no eating in front of siblings
- If you're playing a game, allow your siblings to play or put it away

Those are the major rules of respect that these families observe. There aren't any surprises—they just make sense. Next, he records some rules for respecting the house.

- Enter with clean shoes
- No Gymnastics, hide-and-seek, or ball playing in the house
- No door slamming
- All rooms must be cleaned and straightened before bedtime[17]

Again, there aren't a lot of rules; just some good common sense limits that help protect respect. Next, Guarendi shares these families' rules of supervision. These parents, like successful parents everywhere, recognize the natural tension between their children's desire for independence and the need for parental supervision. He found that successful parents "allow children enough rope to feel some independence but not so much that they tangle themselves into hazardous situations." These are some of their rules:

- Stay in the backyard
- Play within sight of a window or within yelling distance of the house
- Go straight home from school unless otherwise prearranged

Here are a few that apply especially to teens:

- Before leaving the house, tell me "who" (you're going with), "where" (you're going), and "when" (you'll be back)

138

- Wake us up when you get home
- No dating before the age of sixteen[18]

When I was a teenager, those rules applied in my house, too. The only one I didn't really observe was "Wake us up when you get home." No matter how late I stayed out, my mother was always up waiting for me. A few times, I tried to stay out so late that I was sure she'd be asleep when I got in, but it never worked. I never understood why she did that until my own son got his drivers license and started staying out late himself.

You may have a few other rules (such as those governing use of the phone or TV), but generally, highly successful parents find that, regarding rules, "fewer is better." Where mutual respect is practiced, a lot of rules are usually not necessary, especially as the children get older. Successful parents understand that rules are temporary tools that teach and uphold the mutual love and respect upon which self-discipline is built. As mutual respect increases in a family (and the children mature) fewer and fewer rules are needed. In fact, a long list of rules may reflect a lack of respect in the family.

For example, cleaning up the family room after you and your friends played there is a mark of respect for the other family members that will use it next, not just a rule. Letting the rest of the family know where you're going when you leave the house shows respect for the feelings and responsibilities of other family members. It reflects a recognition that family members are all connected and dependent on each other. It's more than just a "rule."

Teens often resent the "Who? Where? When?" rule as an attempt to keep track of them and infringe on their independence. When my sons were teens, I tried to consistently tell them where I was going and when I expected to be back whenever I left the house. They seemed to appreciate that and began to imitate that behavior well as they got older! When no one else was around to tell

139

personally, a note or a message on the telephone answering machine was very acceptable. That helped us avoid a lot of hassles, and still keep track of them. Give respect, and expect it back.

"Different" isn't Necessarily Bad...

When my oldest son was in his second year of college, a friend asked me to lunch. His son was about to enter college and he wanted me to give him any tips I might have for him. "He'll change during college. But if the worst thing that happens is that he comes home wearing an earring, don't get upset," I said.

I thought that was good advice, but it turned out not to be the best thing to say at that time. His son was already wearing an earring and he was quite upset about it. That father couldn't see that his son still remained a sensitive, sensible young man—earring and all.

If you have more than one child, it's certain that you have two very different children! Each of our sons is a unique and wonderful individual. They're clearly our sons, but just as clearly unique from each other and from their parents. I'm confident your children fit that same description. They're enough like you to be recognizable, but different enough to sometimes drive you mad!

You may be a "Type A," driven personality who has to accomplish everything on your list that day by noon. Your child may be mellow and laid back. Maybe you are an academic (or athletic) achiever with a child who struggles just to get by. Maybe you sleep late and just get going when the sun goes down, but your child gets up with the rooster! It can be frustrating! Respecting our children means respecting and accepting the wonderful uniqueness that God has given them; differences in temperament, talent, tastes and opinions, just for starters.

Children do develop some "weird" (that's definitely the most accurate description) tastes. And some of their opinions fall into the same category! Highly successful parents try to respect and accept those tastes and opinions whenever possible, recognizing them as part of their child's growing individuality. Often, they're trying out a "fad" or opinion as a way of practicing their judgement and taste. That's part of the excitement (and work) of being young. Successful parents give their children spoken and unspoken guidance as to what good taste is without necessarily being disrespectful.

When my youngest son was in Junior High, the "hair style of the month" was to shave the side of your head and leave the top full. That was often combined with an equally "unique" style of dress: baggy pants that hung so low their underwear showed! I admit that was not my idea of being dressed to go out in public! Recently, I read about a public school that banned that kind of dress as "disruptive" and "disrespectful." I couldn't help thinking what a silly reaction that was! It's certainly "different," but that's the way teens are. They try out new ideas, opinions and dress styles to see how they "fit," just like adults try on clothes before buying. It's the way teens develop a sense of independence and identity. Making a "federal case" out of it is really disrespectful of them, their opinions, tastes, and feelings.

Here are three common sense rules that have been helpful to me in parenting my teens:

Respect People, Not Necessarily Behavior . As they grow, our children won't be perfect. They'll make mistakes and disappoint us now and then. We won't always like what they do or say, but as parents who live by the Golden Rule we'll always love them no matter what, and treat them with the respect they deserve—no matter how they behave.

Respect Doesn't Necessarily Mean Approval. We won't always like what we hear from them. Some of it will be disappointing, some may make us angry, and some will just be puzzling. We may not like their taste in music or clothing at all! But respect means listening and trying to understand, not approval. That kind of respect keeps channels of communication between parents and children open during even the hardest of disagreements.

Different isn't Necessarily Bad, It's Just Different. Whether referring to different cultures and faiths or opinions and tastes, differences can be disturbing. But our children are individuals, created by God to be unique and special. Respecting their individuality means recognizing that they will inevitably be different from us. That's when we have the opportunity to model for them respect for differences, an important life-skill. After all, differences aren't necessarily bad—they're just different.

Keeping The Balance

Love and respect. Freedom and rules. We've got to keep them all in balance. No wonder successful parents sometimes feel like jugglers in the circus. We've always got to keep things so carefully balanced! There's one more important balance that parents who live by the Golden Rule try hard to maintain—a balance of kindness and firmness.

Balancing loving kindness for our children with appropriate, firmly held limits is the key to both maintaining mutual respect and healthy family discipline. Keeping this balance is no easy task, especially if our own parents didn't do it for us when we were growing up.

Some of us grew up in families with parents who were authoritarian. The attitude (often from the father) was "I said it. That settles it. Now do it!" Everything—and everyone—was tightly controlled. We had very little freedom and opportunity to make our own choices and learn from them. Even when we were in high school, we had to fight for every little bit of independence. There were plenty of limits and lots of firmness in our family, but we had a hard time feeling the love and kindness that comes from respect.

Others of us, especially those who grew up in the 60's and early 70's, had parents who were very permissive. They almost seemed disconnected and uncaring. Family life bordered on chaos sometimes and the freedom we had was scary for a child! "Whatever you want is fine. I love you. You decide." Of course they loved us, but it would have been great to have a little firmness and some healthy limits to guide us as we groped through the maze of growing up! That would have respected our needs, too! And maybe we'd have avoided some of the painful mistakes we made.

As in so much of life, balance is vital. Highly successful parents rely on their faith, parenting instincts, and common sense to strike a balance between being authoritarian (big on firmness and control but without much warmth or respect) or permissive (big on "love" without any firmness, guidance or structure). This balance has been called the "authoritative approach" to parenting.[19] It's also the most healthy and successful one. Parents who follow the authoritative approach leave no doubt in their child's mind about who is ultimately responsible for important family decisions. These parents are in control.

There are, however, different types of control. There is a "coercive control" that concentrates on forcing a child to act against his will. Its main concern is to win any power struggles between parent and child. Sometimes, the wisest, most successful parents must do this—especially when the safety of their youngest children is at stake. But it's not their preferred way of acting.

Highly successful parents who practice the Golden Rule would rather employ what has been called "inductive control." This type of control is achieved by explaining to the child, reasoning with the child (as appropriate to the child's age and the situation), and encouraging the child to voluntarily comply before giving them an order. It avoids power struggles whenever possible. After all, parents can ultimately win just about any power struggle. But that means their children will always lose. And who benefits from being a "loser" all the time?[20]

Successful parents learn to use this respectful approach almost instinctively. Your four year-old is playing with a friend in the yard, and when you tell him it's time to come in for a nap, he protests. Of course, he'd rather stay with his friend—wouldn't you? So, what do you do? Sometimes, there's nothing you can do. The play has to be interrupted. But other times, he and his friend can both come in for a cookie before the nap. Or the two of you can plan what fun thing your child will do after the nap, or plan the next time his friend can come over. It's more work, but it also shows respect and consideration for your four year-old.

I tried this approach with my young teenage son. We were facing the seemingly inevitable struggle over keeping a neat room. I was prepared to give him over to his "cave" for four or five years, as long as no health or fire hazards developed. That was too low a standard for his mother, however. It seemed a fight was inevitable.

Then, he began to complain about his "measly allowance." So we negotiated a deal. If his room was reasonably neat and clean on Friday evening when he received his allowance, he got a 33% bonus. If not, he didn't. Since he really wanted that money, he cleaned his room every Friday afternoon. In fact, he discovered that it was easier to keep it reasonably neat during the week than to do a major cleaning on Friday. His room is now livable (given teenage standards!) most of the time. A little "inductive control" can be a useful parental tool!

A Benevolent Monarchy

Though they clearly remain in control and exercise the responsibilities for their children that God gave them, highly successful parents seek out and consider the feelings and opinions of their children (again—in ways appropriate to their ages) when making decisions. This assures children that they are loved and respected while also providing them the security of the appropriate limits that growing children need.

Here's how Michael, the son of a Midwestern family describes his parents' approach:

> My mother and father make the decisions in our family. If it's a decision that directly affects one of us kids, we are asked how we feel about it, but the final decision is always left up to them....When we were young, they always cared about how we felt about something, but thank goodness they freed us from the responsibility and guilt often associated with having to make all our own decisions. We were allowed to be children. As we grew older, we were given increasingly responsible roles in making choices for ourselves, but we were never abandoned to those choices. We could always go back to my parents for help and advice.[21]

You can hear the love and respect that Michael felt from his parents, and the love and respect he has for them! They cared about how he felt. When decisions affected him, they wanted to know what he thought. They listened. Then, they made the decision. As he grew older, he made more and more decisions on his own. In this case, the parents deliberately delegated their authority to their child in his own best interests.

Let's be clear about one thing: *these authoritative parents are leading neither a democracy or a dictatorship.* It might better be termed a "benevolent monarchy," in which mom and dad are the rulers but the children are respected members of the kingdom. When a decision affects any or all of the members, each is asked for an opinion. All feedback is considered, but the final decision belongs to the parents.[22]

"Authoritative" parents regularly seek out and consider the opinions of their children, even if it doesn't change their decision. It's just basic to parenting by the Golden Rule. For example, who of us doesn't appreciate being consulted by our boss, even if they don't always agree?

There are some real pluses to the family of this practice. Giving children a voice in appropriate family matters (family trips, some discretionary purchases, what kind of Christmas tree, etc.) "carries two benefits. In the short term, kids may better accept decisions they were at least consulted about. In the long term , they will see themselves as a valued part of family decisions and indeed of the whole family."[23] As one child put it, "Our opinions matter and that's a sign that we matter."[24]

Family vacations often provide an opportunity for being an "authoritative" but not authoritarian parent. Deciding where to go and for how long becomes a family matter once your children reach the upper elementary years. We've established a family tradition of vacationing at the same place at the same time for the past 20 years, but as our sons grew older, that tradition has survived only by some respectful flexibility. One year, our high school age son wanted a year "off" from the family vacation. He went to stay with his grandparents and work on their farm instead. In recent years, we've included one of our younger son's cousins on the vacation trip so he'll have a ready "friend" to be with.

Curfews, dating, and driving are just some of the issues and decisions parents and teens face together. Taking the authoritative approach is especially sensible. As they grow toward independence, teens need to take more and more responsibility for their own decisions. The most effective and appropriate style is one of listening, negotiation, and compromise (though parents remain the final authority). Teens need and deserve parents who will respect and listen to them, but who can, when necessary, set firm limits to protect them, also.

In this benevolent monarchy, many things are negotiable, but not everything. When I was eighteen and a senior in high school, I wanted to be free of a curfew on weekends. My parents reluctantly agreed. But one thing was not negotiable: church attendance. Their rule was; "You can stay out as long as you want on Saturday night as long as you're awake and in church on Sunday morning." Whether it's church attendance, the use of drugs and alcohol, or other moral issues, some things are not, and never will be, negotiable for parents who live by the Golden Rule. These parents remain in control.

The authoritative (but not authoritarian) style of parenting—whether with children four years old or fourteen—provides a good measure of kindness and respect, enabling children to develop the self respect they need to make healthy (not self-destructive) choices in life. And it balances that kindness with the firmness of appropriate and loving limits so children can learn what those healthy choices are.

Common Sense Confirmed

In fact, experts confirm the success of this style of parenting. They've studied families who've employed all three approaches and found that the authoritative style (balancing kindness and firmness) is clearly the most successful in helping children develop self-confidence and independence.[25]

An authoritarian style (lots of firmness, little kindness) tends to produce children who respect authority (they'd better if they want to survive in that family!) but have a hard time becoming independent adults. They're too dependent on being told what to do in order to mature into people who can confidently make their own decisions.

Children raised by permissive parents (little kindness or firmness) suffer a similar fate. Their parents never really train them to make healthy choices in life so they often grow up unable to be independent, self-disciplined adults.[26]

Authoritative parents live by the Golden Rule. Their discipline combines the best of both styles; a balance of kindness and firmness, love and limits. In that way, they raise children who become mature, successful adults.[27]

Discipline is not only more effective, but it's also easier when you parent by the Golden Rule. "You will not get much more cooperation, politeness and kindness from children than you give. If you are always too busy to help with puzzles, why should they drop everything to set the table? If you will not listen to them, it will be hard to make them listen to you. They will listen more, and better, if you always explain orders (except in emergencies). Answering 'Why should I' with 'Because I say so' teaches nothing they can use on another occasion."[28]

Jack and Judy Baliswick, in their excellent book, *The Family: A Christian Perspective on the Contemporary Home,* conclude that "the actions of God as parent clearly point to a model in which parental love (support) and discipline (control) intertwine to help children develop toward maturity."[29]

Highly successful parents understand that the authoritative approach to parenting best reflects God's parenting style given to us in the Golden Rule. We can't miss the unconditional love, kindness, and support he brings us. But that love and kindness also carries expectations and limits. He "disciplines" us in love, too. God, our heavenly parent, keeps everything in balance. He sets the perfect example for all successful parents to follow. We're to love, respect, and guide our children, balancing kindness and firmness. In parenting, as in all of life, it's wisest to follow the Golden Rule.

Chapter 7

Discipline as Discipling

Some people can find something positive in just about any situation! Take the story of the twin boys.[1] One was always depressed and negative. There always seemed to be big dark clouds hanging over his head. The other twin was just the opposite; always upbeat and positive. He found the silver lining in all those clouds!

The boys' parents put the negative twin in a room full of the newest, most expensive toys and left him alone to play with them. When they returned a 1/2 hour later, they found he had broken all the toys. "They were just going to break anyway," he said. "Might as well get it over with."

Then, they put their positive son in a room full of nothing but smelly horse manure and gave him a shovel. When they returned a 1/2 hour later, they found him whistling happily and busily digging through the pile with a big grin on his face. When his parents asked him why he was so happy, he said, "With all this horse manure, there must be a pony in here somewhere!"

It's not a true story, of course, but it does illustrate an important point: there's a "bright side" to just about everything in life. Many times, we can make a difficult situation bearable, perhaps even pleasant, just by the perspective we bring to it. If there was ever an aspect of parenting that needed the benefit of a positive approach, it's discipline.

What do the terrible twos, toilet training, sibling rivalry, and adolescence all have in common? They all involve questions of discipline and they all evoke negative images of struggles and tensions between parents and children. I see it in the faces and hear it in the questions of the many parents to whom I speak each year. Whether they're parents-to-be, new parents or parents of teens, there's no other topic that evokes such anxiety among them as discipline. "It's a battle every day." "You've got to keep alert. You can't let down one minute." "We've got to show them who's in charge."

Child Development expert Dr. Penelope Leach once asked twenty-five parents to describe "a good disciplinarian." Nineteen of them said "it was someone who gives clear orders and punishes consistently if a child disobeys."[2] Seen in these terms, is it any wonder that discipline is such a negative, unpleasant topic for most parents (and their children, too!). But it shouldn't be. Oh, there will always be conflict and tension between children and their parents. There will always be children who want to assert their growing independence (or just want what they want when they want it). But *highly successful parents are convinced that discipline is not all dark and dreary. It does have a positive aspect.* Parenting doesn't have to be an eighteen year-long battle.

What Discipline Is and Isn't

Highly successful parents understand that there's more to discipline than just "telling children what to do and punishing them when they don't do it."[3] In fact, there is an important distinction between discipline and punishment. The two are fundamentally very different. One is essentially positive, and the other negative. One is a valuable, everyday focus of parents. The other is a rare, regrettable experience. In fact, discipline and punishment are very, very different.

Discipline refers to the education and nurture of children, the cultivation of their mental and moral faculties. It is primarily educational and not punitive. It does not involve punishment as much as it involves corrective measures to help eliminate undesirable behavior and encourage that which is good. Whatever tools of discipline you use (and we'll discuss some in this and the following chapter) should help children identify and resist what is wrong and unwise rather than just punish.

Punishment is, after all, basically negative. Its purpose is to hurt—to inflict pain. It rarely has a positive, restorative or redemptive goal. It may temporarily curtail and deter the wrong, but doesn't teach the right. It doesn't instruct, it doesn't correct, it doesn't train, and it doesn't encourage.

Discipline, on the other hand, is basically training. In biblical terms, it is "training in righteousness." It is gracious, yet firm. It looks forward to future growth rather than focusing on past failures. In that way, it encourages a child to want to do better the next time. Focusing on past failures only discourages. Punishment says, "You blew it again. You're a failure." Discipline says "That wasn't a good choice. Now, how can you do better the next time?"[4] As Penelope Leach says, discipline is all about "helping children grow into people who will one day do as they should and behave as they ought when there's nobody around to tell, supervise or punish them."[5] When you look at discipline that way, it really is much more positive.

Apprenticing for Life

There's an old saying that if you don't know where you're going, that's exactly where you'll end up! It's a reminder of the importance of having clear, long term goals in mind to guide us. Having a long term goal for our parenting helps us keep moving toward being highly successful parents even on those days when teasing and tantrums throw up roadblocks! It helps us stay focused on the "big picture" when the little things of daily life threaten to overwhelm us.

What is your goal as a parent? Have you clearly defined what you want your children to be like when they grow up and how you can prepare them for that? If not, let me suggest this one: *The goal of parents is to prepare their children to live as mature, independent, productive adults who have a firm moral and spiritual capacity, are capable of loving and being loved, and will leave the world a little better place for having lived.*

Sounds ambitious, doesn't it? What it really boils down to is that, from the day we bring them home from the hospital to the day they leave to set up their own home, our goal is to prepare them for successful, independent living. Discipline is a process of guiding our children to maturity. That process takes time. Fortunately, most of us get at least eighteen years to do it!

How do successful parents reach their goal? They give their children a good example to follow (remember the conviction that "Good Parenting begins with Good Personing") and guide them carefully as they practice and learn during the period we call "growing up." It may not be easy, but it's not all toil and trouble either! It's an adventure. It's a privilege. It's a gift.

Do you remember when you first "helped" your mother bake? Perhaps she guided your hand as you measured the flour or showed you how to put the batter in the pan. As you grew older, she left you to do more and more of it yourself. She'd be there to remind you if you forgot an ingredient or to help if you had a problem. Later, she'd let you do it yourself, just checking-in once in a while to see how it was going. That's still how many young people learn baking, auto maintenance and other skills today. It's a process known as apprenticing.

Throughout the middle ages and up until the beginning of the Industrial Revolution, the apprenticeship system was the common way most young people learned the skills of living. A young person might be apprenticed to a baker, cobbler, or other tradesman. By watching, listening, and practicing under adult guidance, they gradually learned the skills needed to become an economically independent adult. I doubt if the apprenticeship was always a happy time. The youth made mistakes and lost their patience now and then, I'm sure. So did their master. But in spite of those problems, it was largely a positive process. Both master and apprentice shared a good goal: passing on to the youth the skills needed to be a productive adult.

Popular television programs such as *Little House on the Prairie* or *The Waltons* showed how, in earlier days, young people worked along side their parents in the fields or in the house learning the skills they'd later need to survive on their own. By observing Charles Ingalls or Papa Walton in the daily business of life, their children not only learned economic skills, but also values such as patience, kindness, honesty, integrity, hard work, faith, and how to get along with others. Life was certainly their best (and sometimes, their only) teacher. And they had the opportunity to practice these skills and values while a caring adult guided them.

When I was growing up on my parents' daily farm, I learned to do the farm chores by working right along side my dad. At milking time and in the fields, he saw that I learned to do my tasks well and to see them through to completion. Those qualities were important to the success of the farm, and he knew they would be important to me throughout my life as an adult. I learned to be disciplined like most children through much of history—by observing and working alongside my parents. Today, we may not be teaching our children vocational skills, but our role as parents is quite similar. Our children are under our apprenticeship to learn

CONFIDENT PARENTING IN CHALLENGING TIMES

how to live. They watch and listen and practice. We instruct, demonstrate, guide, support, and protect.

Children today have many more vocational choices than children even a century ago. They can, and likely will, choose a different career than we did. But Jay Kessler, the President of Taylor University, observes that, regardless of their career choices, they will probably become like us in the area of values. He says that the question successful parents must constantly ask themselves is, "How can I perform in a competent, mature manner so that when my kids copy me, I'll be happy with what I observe in them?"[6] *Wise (and highly successful) parents don't focus on perfecting their child's behavior as much as on perfecting their own.*[7]

Under our apprenticeship, our children aren't learning to make a product, they're learning how to live. They aren't watching what we make, they're watching us. They don't copy our workmanship, they copy our lives.

Discipling Our Children

In spiritual terms, we call this process "discipleship." The words "disciple" and "discipline" come from the same root word meaning instruction or teaching. The process of disciplining our children involves not only patiently teaching or telling them what to believe, but also how to behave. As we've seen, it means demonstrating or modeling responsible behavior. It means gently guiding them as they practice making choices, which includes failing, learning from the consequences, and trying again. During this process we continue to give our children the unfailing love and care they need and deserve from us.[8]

The key to living successfully, and to finding the silver lining in the many dark clouds of life, is a firm faith. And there's no more effective way for parents to give their children that faith than teaching them through the daily experiences of life. "Virtually all spiritual lessons come from living with one another, especially with parents. In one sense, the entire relationship parents have with children is a process of Christian Education."[9]

After all, how do children learn what it means to love someone except by being loved? How do they learn when and how to forgive others except in the daily quarrels and squabbles of the family? How do they learn the meaning and value of faith and honesty more effectively than by experiencing it at home? And there is no better way to learn what it means to be a citizen of the Kingdom of God than by living with their parents and seeing how they relate to God.[10]

Of course, a "religious" home is not necessarily a Christian one. A "religious" home will not necessarily bring faith to children. A discipling home is characterized by what I have elsewhere called a Christian "family atmosphere."[11]— where the parents' faith is evident throughout and "the family's values are as vital to them as the air they breathe, the water they drink and the food they eat. Values are just as important in the daily activities of work and play as they are in moments of crucial decisions."[12] In other words, every day of family life presents opportunities for parents to help their children see and appreciate the presence and activity of God and to learn to respond to him.

Does that mean parents have to be perfect? Hardly. We know too well that it's not possible. But what really matters to our children, especially our teens, is not that we're perfect but that we're real people who "walk our talk," admit our failures, and keep on trying. The life of faith, like life in general, is not all success. But even our failures can be means to teaching our children important life lessons. So as we disciple our children spiritually, we can let them see our struggles and failures. That way, they can learn the invaluable lesson that the best way to deal with failure "is to let the strong arms of God embrace and redeem us, and then go forward again."[13]

Follow God's Example

For many parents, this is a very different approach to discipline than they grew up with. Some of us grew up in families where discipline was more about "who's the boss?" than getting prepared for life. Others remember only long lists of rules to be obeyed and harsh punishment. How can we shake these negative images and replace them with a positive approach to discipline?

The place to start is with the example of God, our heavenly father. God's discipline isn't about power (although he's got plenty of it). Its goal isn't behavior control (although some of that is certainly necessary). God's discipline is about what has been called "empowering" his children to maturity—to be all they were intended to be.[14] God's empowering is motivated by his unconditional love for us. Our empowering of our children is motivated by that same unconditional love, "love that is unaffected by a child's misbehavior." As one wise mother observed, "When your children are acting the worst, that's when they need your love the most."[15]

God sets limits and boundaries for us, but their purpose is always positive and loving: to teach us how to live. He allows us freedom to make our own choices, but even when we fail, he is ready to forgive us and help us learn from our failures. He doesn't abandon us, but looks forward with us to the future. His goal for us is that we grow and mature to be all that he created us to be.

Following God's example, highly successful parents "empower" their children using this same, positive approach to discipline. They focus most on what their children do right, not wrong.[16] In that way, they build up their children, enhancing their self-esteem so they can become competent in knowing what is right and confident in choosing it. One successful mother put it this way: "When you tell your children the good you see in them, they are a little less afraid to test it on others."[17]

156

Empowering helps children recognize their strengths and build on them. It sets a standard for children to live up to, not to fall down to. It looks forward to future growth, not backward to past mistakes. It says to a child "You're so very loved and special. I want only the best for you in life. Here is the best I can give you. Choose nothing less! And, remember, I'm always here to help you." What a powerful, positive message to give a growing child!

Instead of wondering "What's the best way to discipline my child?" try asking a more positive question: "How can I help my child become a responsible adult in the same way God is teaching me?" When you look at discipline as discipling your children, and preparing them for successful adulthood, it becomes an exciting, positive process.[18] On those days when tantrums and teasing threaten to overwhelm them, highly successful parents remember that the dark cloud of discipline really does have a silver lining!

Putting It All To Work

So far, we've talked a lot about this positive approach to discipline. Now, it's time to see how it applies to the every day process of preparing our children for life. Here are seven keys to everyday discipline on which successful parents rely.

1. Think positively!

Do you remember the story of the twin boys at the beginning of this chapter? So much in life is effected by the perspective we bring to it. Highly successful parents see the big picture and let their understanding of discipline, based on God's parenting, shape their daily relationship with their children. A positive perspective isn't always easy— especially when your two year-old is sick and your four year-old is cranky, or the ten year-old is pouting and your teen is whining. But that's exactly when we need to think positively. Sometimes, it just takes effort and some creativity!

That's the lesson of this humorous story:[19] Early one week, a pastor received a call from a man in his congregation telling him that the man's brother had died. He asked the pastor to conduct the funeral.

"There's just one request I have, Pastor," the man said. "I know my brother didn't lead the greatest life, but he's gone now. It would mean a lot to me if, during your remarks, you'd call him a saint. And to show my appreciation, I'll donate $1000 to your building fund."

That put the pastor in a terrible bind. The man who had died was a real scoundrel. His life was no model for anyone. But the pastor knew that the building fund needed the money. He struggled and agonized over his dilemma. Somehow, he had to do it. He had to be positive about this man and find a way to call him a saint.

By the day of the funeral, he'd found a creative way to solve his problem. "We know that John did not lead a perfect life," the pastor said. "He made a lot of mistakes, to be sure. But he was a saint compared to his brother." And the pastor got his $1000.

It's a funny story with a good lesson. Sometimes, it takes a lot of work and creativity to be positive about discipline. So, it helps to keep in mind what we've learned about discipline so far. It's not punishment. It's not primarily imposing our will on our children, regardless of their needs or feelings. Rather, it's a "process of learning and guidance that is based on respect for your child."[20]

We parents are discipling our children; giving them positive guidance through both our words and actions.[21] Discipling employs this positive approach to educating and training children for life. It is forward looking and encouraging. Keeping that in mind helps you find the silver lining in even the most difficult discipline situation.

2. Love with limits.

"All you need is love" is a romantic, highly appealing notion. But, successful parents know that when it comes to raising children, love is not enough to prepare a child well for life. Love needs to be complemented by discipline, respect, and hard work!

Teaching, modeling, and enforcing repeatedly and consistently are hard work! Loving our children means doing our very best for them in the relatively few years we have to train them. And highly successful parents understand that there aren't any "shortcuts." It's just common sense that "You get back what you put in."

Highly successful parents believe that unconditional love includes limits or rules (another way to describe discipline). "Real love means we're kind and compassionate, while also firm and fair. In fact, we can't have real love for our children without reasonable, healthy limits to guide and nurture them."[22]

As Dr. Kevin Lehman wisely points out, limits aren't conditions on your love; "limits help channel your love and give it the substance that makes it real and lasting, not artificial and temporary." Of course, limits (or rules) and the consequences for breaking them can make your child feel unloved. That's why a positive approach, built around a partnership (with the parent being the "senior" partner) together with plenty of hugs, encouragement and kindness, is so important. It's this rich love that makes discipline effective.[23]

Successful parents know the value of working hard at this kind of discipline. They are willing to do whatever it takes to discipline their children today so that life won't discipline them tomorrow. They're loving, which includes being firm, because they're convinced that even "the firmest parent, if loving, is a more gentle teacher than the world. For a child's sake, parents need the will to discipline."[24] Love with no limits is not enough. Love includes limits.

3. Observe the "Two Ears, One Mouth" rule.

There's an old saying that "God gave us two ears and one mouth so we could listen twice as much as we speak." That's advice that highly successful parents follow. They know how crucial it is to really listen to their children.

"Listening is one of the most valuable things we can do for another person," says Fred Rogers of TV's "Mister Rogers' Neighborhood." "A child's communications should be received as one would a gift—with tact and gratitude—even on those occasions when the 'gift' is ill-chosen or not what one had hoped for. Listening to those we love can be our greatest gift to them."[25] This includes listening to our children!

It makes sense that children can talk more if parents listen more. *So highly successful parents listen by first being quiet.* One father says that, for him, good listening means keeping his mouth shut until his child closes hers![26] That's often the hardest part of listening, isn't it? We parents often have to fight the temptation to stop listening and cut off our child with some advice or correction.

Our youngest son is a real "people person." He likes nothing better than being surrounded at all times by lots of friends. As a child, he'd often come into the house upset or angry over a fight with his friends. Since he was still learning how to get along with others, my wife and I wanted to take advantage of those teachable moments. We quickly learned that if our first reaction was "What did you expect? That wasn't a very kind thing to do!" or a similar unsympathetic remark, we only made him more upset and unwilling to listen to us at all. The teachable moment was lost!

When we listen to our child's point of view, they're more likely to feel that we're on their side. Then, they'll be more willing to listen to what we have to say. My wife and I learned that it wasn't until we had listened and been appropriately supportive and sympathetic to our son, that he was willing to listen to our advice and correction.

160

Both common sense and love say "you don't kick a person when he's down." If a child's every attempt to share a problem or frustration is interrupted with "But why didn't you do it right the first time?" or "Haven't I told you before how foolish that is?" soon there won't be any more sharing! It's too dangerous. It just ends up in a fight.

In the same way, successful parents know the value of not criticizing their children's beliefs and opinions too quickly or harshly. "Nothing shuts up a kid faster than an adult who tramples his ideas. Would *you* reveal your hopes and concerns to someone who consistently told you what was wrong with them?"[27] When they need to help their children learn "a better way," successful parents first look for something to affirm about their child's opinion or values, and then calmly say something like, "Have you thought about it this way?" That helps children see their parents' perspectives while keeping communications open.

Some good advice for parents is found in the ancient wisdom of the Book of Proverbs: "If one gives an answer before hearing, it is folly and shame."[28] In other words, "Listen as long as you can. There's no rush to talk. You'll hear more of what a child is thinking and when you do speak, you'll speak with more understanding and ability."[29]

Listen for Feelings

Successful parents know that listening to their children means hearing feelings as well as words. "I guess that really made you angry, didn't it?" or "It sounds as if you are really disappointed right now" are statements that show we've really tried to listen to what they've told us and that we understand their feelings (even if we disagree with them!). Taking the time to really know how our children think and feel helps produce love and closeness.

Good listening, like most other important things in family life, requires being available. As children become teens, they become less dependent on their parents and tend to confide more in friends, so being available to listen when they want to talk is crucial. In our house, "talk time" was often those few minutes when they first came in the door after school (after the trip to the refrigerator, of course) or at bedtime. When he was in high school, our oldest son often dropped by our bedroom to talk late in the evening. So sometimes, we purposely stayed awake, expecting him to come by to talk. And we were always ready to listen when he did!

With young children, bedtime is often a time of special closeness. They're ready and eager to talk about their experiences and feelings. Sure, this could be a stalling tactic, but not always. And even if it is, just allow for a few minutes of talk time when you set a bedtime. It's time well spent.

The youngest children are less able to organize their thoughts so it often takes them longer to express them in a way that we parents can understand. That requires not just listening, but listening *patiently*[30] Sometimes the matter isn't that urgent (except to a three year-old!). Sometimes, we really are too busy to listen. At those times, you can still say "Let's talk about this during dinner" (or "at bedtime" or "at 4 P.M., when I'm finished"). The important thing is that *highly successful parents listen to their children at least as much as they talk to them.* Through patient, loving listening, they build a bond of intimacy that enables them to both know their children and successfully disciple them.

4. <u>Give them something to "live up to."</u>
As my sons and I stood at my father's graveside after his funeral, we recalled the many kind words people had said about him during the service. They were words such as "integrity," "faithfulness" and "service." "Your grandfather left us quite a standard to live up to," I told my sons. We all knew it was true. And we all wanted to live up to it.

Educators have known it for years. Highly successful parents know it, too. *Children live up (or down) to the expectations we have for them and the standards we set for them.* So successful parents keep both expectations and standards high. After all, if they don't expect the best from their children, who will? Highly successful parents are convinced that every child is born with great potential. So they tell their children how special they are and then encourage them to develop to the fullest of their potential. "Settling for average in morals, manners, or character is not something these parents are comfortable doing."[31]

We've probably all seen a neighbor's three year-old who can count to one thousand, recite the alphabet backwards and play Mozart on the piano. Highly successful parents want their children to achieve, also. But they reject the idea that "the child who goes the fastest goes the farthest." They resist the temptation to hurry their child into premature achievements or miniature adulthood. Instead, they allow their children to be children and to grow at their own pace.

Highly successful parents judge their success "by the warmth and honesty of their child's relationships [and] by the depth and morality of their principles...," not mainly by their child's achievements.[32] As David Elkind wisely observes, "success in life is not the product of acquired academic skills; rather success in life is the product of a healthy personality."[33] That is what highly successful parents want first for their growing children.

Faced with a neighbor's high achieving toddler, we mutter "My child is just as smart and talented as theirs." And they probably are, but they may be in different areas. Or maybe they won't ever be a nuclear physicist, but they're one of those children that people just love to have around them. Successful parents encourage and support their children to achieve, but maintain realistic expectation and standards. They expect their children to do *their* best and no more; to achieve to the best of *their* ability, whatever that

163

may be. Excellence is measured by their own standards—not anyone else's.

Keep Your Expectations Realistic

Successful parents are realistic, also. Whether regarding achievements or self-discipline, they liberally sprinkle their high expectations for their children with a healthy dose of realism. They expect the best of their children, but not beyond the realistic limits of their capability.

We live in upstate New York where it's snowy in the winter and muddy in the spring. At least in our house, four and five year-old boys never seemed to be able to consistently wipe their boots or shoes before coming in the house. That snack they were after just seemed to capture all their attention! My wife and I learned to keep reminding them and to be pleased with the times they did remember, but not to expect perfection.

If you expect a toddler to never play with her food or a four year-old to never track in some dirt, you'll surely be disappointed! Your expectations just aren't realistic! After all, if they were perfectly well disciplined, they wouldn't be children—they'd be adults just like us!

Given that our children won't always meet our standards and expectations, how do we help their best get better and better? "Let no goodness go unnoticed," one mother says.[34] Another way to say it is, "Catch them doing good." Whenever their child *does* clean his shoes before coming in the house, *does* remember to feed the pet, *does* keep her room neat or *does* let you know where they're going when they leave the house, Mom or Dad are sure to offer praise. They know that praise encourages similar good behavior in the future.

There's an old common sense saying that "You catch more flies with honey than with vinegar." Praise is a more

164

effective motivator than criticism. Highly successful parents try to focus on what their children do right, not wrong. They focus on the positive. The praise it and they reinforce it.

"I appreciate your helpfulness today" is much more effective in encouraging a child to repeat her good behavior than "Well, it's about time you remembered!" "You're doing much better" will more effectively encourage a child to keep trying than "What's the matter with you! It's still not right." This kind of a positive, encouraging approach is not only good for a child's self-image, but is usually more effective in helping them develop self-discipline.

More than once, one of my sons came home from school and complained of a confrontation with a teacher or classmate. Often, my wife or I said, "What did you do to provoke him?" or "You must have been really acting up today." We assumed the worst. Sometimes, it was true, but far from always. As I listened and investigated, I found that, often, the situation wasn't entirely my son's fault. I learned to sympathize, listen carefully, and try to get the whole picture before jumping to negative conclusions. "When you automatically assume that your child is at fault or has misbehaved...you send him a message that he is intrinsically bad."[35]   That's not the message we want to send our children!

We're On Your Side

In the story of the twin boys, the little boy locked in the room with loads of new, exciting toys assumed they would all end up broken. And what was the result? He soon sat in a room full of broken toys. His expectations were realized. Most of what children hear from adults today centers on their problems and failures. We're quick with criticism and slow with praise. Psychologist James Windell says, "If you only point out ways in which kids fall short of expectations, failure becomes a self-fulfilling prophecy."[36] How much better it would be if children heard more "positive reminders that, regardless of their failures, they are moving in the right direction."[37]

Successful parents know that "children will be children" and they will sometimes fail to meet even the most realistic expectations. They are not easily surprised or overly upset, but rather are reasonable when their children fail and determined to help them do better in the future. Many days, it takes all the faith they have, but *successful parents give their children this very positive message: "We believe in you. We know you can do it. And we know you'll do better the next time."* This encouragement and faith are strong incentives to a child or teen to live up to the expectations their parents have for them. "The one thing all parents can do for their child is to believe in them. This belief and confidence can take kids through times of discouragement when they really want to give up on a task or give in to temptation."[38]

Whatever else they say or do, successful parents want their children to know one thing: "We're on your side." They don't dwell on their children's past failures (who likes to be reminded of them?), but encourage their children to keep moving ahead to do better in the future because they know that *children who are encouraged and trusted are motivated to behave responsibly.*[39] And if children don't feel that their parents expect and believe the best for them and from them, how can they believe it for themselves?

As we've already seen, if we want our children to do their best, in manners, morals or achievements, we must set the example. A young man named Michael explained how his parents did it. "My parents believed that you get what you expect from a child and they expected a lot from us. But they never asked anything of us unless they set the example we were to follow. They practiced what they preached."[40]

Someone has wisely observed that children need models, not critics. Critics are all around them. Loving, consistent models to whom they can look for encouragement and guidance are rare.   What children need from their parents is an example to follow.   You can do this for your children.   "Train up a child in the way he should go and walk that way yourself once in a while" is the way one person humorously put it.   Highly successful parents act as models for their children, not critics.   They give them something to "live up to"!

5. Be a "Yes" parent.

It's the one word that comes to a parent's lips the quickest.   Whenever a young child wants to do something it almost always requires a parent's help, and whatever it is, their request always seems to come at just the wrong time.   We're too busy, too tired, too late or too "something."   So we say "No."

Sometimes, there are very good reasons for saying "No."   A three year-old doesn't understand limitations of cost or safety.   Sometimes, we just want to protect our child from getting hurt or being disappointed (and we know we'll be the one to have to pick up the pieces).   Sometimes, "No" really is for a child's own good.

But if you're like me, you have to admit that two letter word is often uttered more for convenience than anything else.   When your child wants to play out in the snow (after you've just cleaned the house), have a friend over (with all the commotion that brings), make a cake with you (and an even bigger mess), or go to a pajama party (and stay up who knows how late!), your first reaction may be to say "No" unless they can nag and whine you into agreement.

When my younger son was in elementary school, his idea of a good Friday night was to have a friend sleep over.   And he soon wanted to have a sleep-over every weekend!   Inevitably, he and his friend would laugh loudly, wrestle wildly, and finally go to sleep.   Then, they'd start all over again early Saturday morning while my wife and I tried to enjoy our one day to sleep in. It wasn't long before I started saying "No" to all requests for Friday night sleepovers.

He and I had some heated discussions over this (alright, they were arguments). Enjoying his friends one-on-one really was important to my son. On a relatively quiet day, I recognized that their noise was really just a minor inconvenience to me. I really did want to find a way to say "Yes" to his requests. So we arrived at a simple and satisfactory compromise. Overnights could be allowed every other weekend. That seemed fair to us both. Then, I was able to say "Yes" to his sleep-over requests.

When we're constantly saying "No" to our children, no matter what their age or request, parenting becomes an endless series of confrontations and arguments ("Why can't I?" "Because I said so!" "You can't stop me!" "You'd better watch yourself, young man!") instead of an apprenticeship for living. Discipline becomes an exercise in control ("keeping the lid on") rather than discipling. Power struggles and a generally negative atmosphere quickly take over the family.

No Winner, Only Losers

Power struggles aren't always avoidable, but they're always regrettable. When your toddler insists on running into the street, you've got to assert control—their life is at stake. When your teen insists on abusing himself with drugs or alcohol, you've got to assert control—their life is at stake. *Highly successful parents know when to take control, and they do it.*

But many times, power struggles can be avoided. And sometimes, what looks like a power struggle may not be one at all. At one of my recent parenting seminars, a frustrated mother told me of her four year-old daughter who just wouldn't stay in her room and go to sleep after her mother turned the lights out. "I put her to bed, but she keeps coming out of her room and saying she isn't sleepy. I've tried putting her back in the room and threatening her with a spanking but nothing seems to work."

The mother seemed surprised when I suggested to her that maybe her daughter really wasn't tired. "What does she like most about bedtime?," I asked the mother. "She likes reading her books." So I suggested that she be allowed to stay in her bed with the light on and read her books until she was ready to fall asleep. But if she got out of bed, the lights went out and the books were put away. I was pretty sure that when she got tired enough, she'd fall asleep. That way, her mother could move on to her other evening responsibilities, and the daughter could go to sleep when she was tired. Left by herself with no distractions or stimulation, that's what would happen, I was sure. If it worked, there'd be no more power struggles, and everybody wins!

During the seminar, the mother said she was ready to try locking the girl in her room or spanking her repeatedly each evening until she stayed in bed. Those strategies might have worked in the sense of the mother winning, but at what cost? *Highly successful parents are convinced that the trouble with power struggles is that there are no winners, only losers.*

Any parents can win a struggle with a young child if the parent is determined enough. But successful parents know that no child benefits from always being a loser. It eats away at their self-esteem. It builds up frustration, anger and resentment. When family life becomes a series of unending power struggles between parents who always say "No" and children who need to feel some bit of independence and control over their lives, or who want some recognition of their needs and wishes, everybody loses. Parents lose the respect of their children and the joy of parenting. Children lose self-respect and the benefit of learning by doing under the guidance and protection of their parents.

As long as parents are simply trying to win, they're trying to make losers out of their children. But the goal of highly successful parents is far, far different. *"Our goal is to win children over, not to win over children."*[A1] By our unconditional love and respect for our children, we strive to "win them over" to the mature, responsible manner of living we're teaching and modeling for them. "Winning over children" through constant power struggles that "show who's the boss" undermines discipling. And in the long run, it simply won't work.

Say "Yes" Whenever Possible

Highly successful parents are "Yes" parents. Being a "Yes" parent is a way of avoiding unnecessary power struggles. It not only means saying "Yes" whenever possible, but giving choices and acceptable alternatives when "No" is clearly called for.

I learned that lesson with my foster daughter. It was amazing how, at five or six years old, she seemed to know how to ask for just the wrong thing at just the wrong time! I was constantly saying "No" to her and neither of us was enjoying each other very much. I shared my frustration with another parent one day and he suggested I not just say "No," but whenever possible, tell her that there was something she could do. He called it a "qualified 'No.'" He suggested I try to say something like, "That won't work right now, but how about doing this or this?" I gave her a choice of acceptable (at least to me) alternatives and avoided the "N" word, whenever I could. Sometimes, all it takes is a choice (or an acceptable alternative) to satisfy a child and avoid an unnecessary power struggle.

Successful "Yes" parents use alternatives to "No" whenever possible. For example, instead of simply saying to your child "No, you can't splash in the water in the sink," you can say, "Let's play in the water in the bathtub. That's the best place to play in the water." Or "This isn't a good time to go outside, but what else would be fun to do right now?"

"Yes parents" try to state limits in a positive way, also. Often, that makes them more palatable to a child and teaches not only what isn't allowed, but, equally importantly, what is. So instead of just "No, you may not interrupt when I'm speaking," you might say "It's polite to wait until I'm finished talking before you talk. If you stand there quietly, I'll know you want to talk to me." Or "Let's be sure all your toys are in their box before you go to bed" instead of "Don't leave your toys in a mess on the floor every night."

Additionally, your "No" loses its effectiveness if it's overused. Either your children stop listening and really hearing it, or you can't stick to all your "Nos" and they stop believing you.[42] Better to save your "Nos" for those times when you really need them. Because "Yes parents" say "Yes" whenever possible, their children trust that a "No" must really be necessary and their parents really do mean it.

Teens Need Responsibility

Teens rightly ask for, and need to take, increasing responsibility for their lives. So highly successful parents give their teens more and more responsibility as they mature and rely increasingly on discussions, negotiation and compromise to set limits.

One successful parent said her children have no bedtime or curfews. Her children go to sleep when they're tired. "If they fall asleep in school, then we have a problem, which we'll deal with. But they aren't dumb—they know that if they fall asleep during the day, it's because they're staying up too late at night. So they'll give me a sheepish grin and decide to go to bed earlier."[43]

This same mother had an 11:00 P.M. curfew for her teenage daughter for awhile, but regularly there seemed to be good reasons (school activities, trips with other families, for example) for coming in later. So the family dropped that "arbitrary rule" and decided to discuss each situation separately to arrive at a reasonable time for the daughter to be home.

When my oldest son was sixteen, I didn't want to set a firm curfew for him for similar reasons. Events such as movies or school functions had different ending times, meaning we'd have to negotiate a specific time to be home, anyway. Often, as he was getting ready to leave, I'd ask him "When do you plan to be home?" More often than not, I got an acceptable answer and said, "Fine. I'll expect see you then. If you have a problem, just give me a call." That way, he took responsibility for setting his own curfew and observing it. If his suggested arrival time wasn't satisfactory, we'd negotiate one that was.

A similar approach works well with disputes. If your teen wants to do something you don't approve of, discussion and negotiation can be very positive. You can share your concerns with your teen (an education for them!) and ask them what suggestions they have for dealing with them. Often, they come up with acceptable suggestions or compromises (he'll let you know where he "ends up," he'll bring her here instead of going to her place alone, she'll pay for it herself). When they do, it's no longer your restrictions that have bound them, but their solutions.

"Yes parents" understand that negotiation and compromise help children to learn important skills of living and to feel respected at the same time. Whether the issue is clothing, curfews, driving or dating, parents of teens know that negotiation and compromise is a necessary tool. They do pick their battles carefully, but because they love their children, they don't shrink from the really important ones. Where serious issues of morality, legality, health and safety are concerned, even a "Yes" parent will firmly say "No." They balance their love with firm and clear limits.

In one of his "Focus on The Family" Radio commentaries, Dr. James Dobson made the case for being a "Yes" parent very persuasively. This is how he put it: "No, you can't go out. No, you can't have a cookie. No, you can't use the telephone. And no, you can't go to Susie's house. No, no, no, no. How many times each day do we use that small but powerful word with our children?"[44]

As parents we could say "Yes" to most routine requests made by our kids. But we often choose, almost automatically, to respond in the negative. Why? Because we don't want to take the time to stop and think about the consequences; because the activity would cause us more work or physical effort; because there might be danger in the request; and because we know our children ask a thousand favors every day, and it's just more convenient to refuse them all.

Now, it's true that every child needs to be acquainted with denial of some of his or her more extravagant wishes, but we must not fall into the habit of turning down reasonable requests from our kids. Our children already face so many "Nos" in life that we should say "Yes" whenever we can. "And it's good to ask ourselves every once in a while: *How do my children view me? As an oppressive judge and jury? As a demanding boss? Or do they think of me as a loving parent who is, above all else, fair and just in our daily interaction?* One way to build a healthy relationship is to say 'Yes' unless there is a very good reason to do otherwise."[45]

That's some good, common sense advice. Do you want to be a "Yes" parent? Here's the rule I try to follow in my family. *"Say 'Yes' unless, not 'No' until"* . *Try to say "Yes" to your child's requests unless there's a good reason not to rather than saying "No" until they can convince you otherwise.* This approach helps minimize confrontations, power struggles, whining and all sorts of problems. It helps make discipline, and family life in general, a lot more positive. Highly successful parents are "Yes" parents.

6. Remember that "practice makes perfect"

Do you remember the old story about the man who approached a cab driver in New York for directions? "How do you get to Carnegie Hall?" the man asked. The cab driver replied, "That's easy. Practice, Practice, Practice!"

Learning to do anything well usually requires practice. Learning to live successfully as an adult is no exception. But living is different from playing the violin or flute. For an adult, daily life is a series of choices. Some are pretty big ones. Where will I work? How will I spend my money? Will I get married? Will I have children? How will I grow spiritually? Other choices are relatively minor. What clothes will I wear today? What will I do for my vacation? What will I have for dinner? But big or small, choices have to be made. The skill of making good choices, big or small, is learned through practice. We make choices, see the consequences, learn from our failures and successes and move ahead to the next one.

God's plan for parents is that they "work themselves out of a job" by preparing their children for responsible, independent living. Highly successful parents understand that children get better at things they practice. Likewise, "they believe that children must have responsibility if they are to become responsible, that they must make their own decisions if they are to learn good judgement."[46] So they begin allowing their children to practice making age appropriate choices early in life and continue that until their children leave home. At first the choices are very simple. You might allow your three year-old to decide which of two shirts to wear today or which of two or three playmates to invite over to play for the afternoon. By ten or eleven, the same child may be allowed to choose when to do homework (after school or after dinner) and have wide freedom over what to wear to school.

When children are given appropriate choices, they learn an important lesson: "I'm responsible for choosing and for what happens as a result. So I'd better choose carefully."

Such choices are not a threat to a parent's authority. After all, who gave the child the choices? One advantage to giving a child appropriate choices is that it puts responsibility right where it belongs; on the child. "I'm sorry about your friend wanting to come over tonight, but you did chose to do your homework after dinner. Maybe she can come over tomorrow." There's less need for nagging. After all, who's choice was it to do homework after dinner?[47]

As children progress through the teen years, their choices grow more serious. By the mid-teens, children generally choose their own friends (whether we like them or not!). They begin to demand choices about where and when they go, what they do, and who they do it with. They make academic and vocational choices, as well as choices about personal conduct, values, and faith.

How do successful parents "disciple" or discipline children in the mid to late teen years? Most often, they do it by taking on the role of a coach or mentor. They give their children directions less and less, and they provide advice and encouragement (and, whenever necessary, clear limits) more and more. Most importantly, highly successful parents give their teens more and more freedom to practice making many everyday choices. In other words, their parents trust them.

I'll Trust You Until...

"But you don't trust me" is an all-too-common teenage complaint. Nothing is more important to our children than feeling that we trust them. And nothing is more crucial to their success in learning to make wise choices than our trust. Do you remember our fourth key to discipline, "Give Them Something to Live 'Up To'"? Our trust gives them something to live up to as they make their own choices. Sometimes, we don't really *want* to trust our children. We're not sure they're really trustworthy. Giving them the trust they need can be pretty scary!

175

"You have to show kids how to be trustworthy. They have to know what it is that makes you trust them, so that they can cultivate and trust those things in themselves. Before trust can exist, a child has to know what his or her parents mean by good judgement or moral behavior." *So highly successful parents understand that they can trust their children's judgement because they've shown them how to make good decisions. They trust their morals because they've raised them in a moral environment.* And they've helped them practice those skills "by allowing them to make decisions and assume responsibility as they mature."[48]

That's how discipling or apprenticeship works. Successful parents model the values and responsibility they want their children to develop. "It is the way [parents] live, rather than the rules they set, that maintains 'discipline.'"[49]

I think my oldest son was about fifteen when I said this to another adult. I intentionally said it while my son was listening. "I don't worry about him. I'll trust him until he gives me reason not to." That became my rule with my son during his teenage years. *"I'll trust you until you give me reason not to."* I gave him trust to live up to. It was a gift. He didn't have to earn it. It was his until he lost it. He never did.

Does trusting our children with choices mean expecting they'll never make mistakes? Of course not. But they do need our trust in order to develop into self-disciplined adults. So successful parents trust their children "to mean well even when they don't do well."[50] After all, "practice makes perfect." They don't start out perfect, but as they keep practicing, and learning from their mistakes, they do get better!

The School of Hard Knocks

Management Expert Tom Peters isn't known for advice on parenting, but he recognizes the value of letting children assume gradual responsibility for their behavior and make their own mistakes. "Skillful parenting," he says, "hinges on letting go." Successful parents assign their children responsibility for their behavior and let them make mistakes because they know that some of the most valuable of life's lessons are learned by trial and error.[51]

One of those valuable lessons that every child must learn is that all of our actions (and the choices that lead to them) have consequences. If you make certain choices, certain unpleasant results usually follow. If you don't wear proper clothing in the winter when you go outside to play, you'll be cold and probably have to stop playing and come in to dress more warmly. If you don't eat enough at mealtime, you'll be hungry long before the next one. If you are unkind to others, you won't have many friends.

When my youngest son got to be about eleven, I decided to stop nagging him about wearing a warm coat to school. He was old enough to make his own choice. If he was cold waiting for the bus, he could come back in if he had time. If not, he'd be cold that day. I was certain he'd learn a valuable lesson from that mistake. There'd be no need for me to nag.

When safety is not an issue, letting children make their own choices, take responsibility for their behavior and learn from their mistakes (the "School of Hard Knocks") is the most effective way to prepare them for life. While they are young and under our care, we can still give them good advice and, in the most serious cases, protect them from dangerous choices. But if we don't let them learn from their mistakes (those with relatively minor consequences) when they are young, "reality will teach them when they are older, and by then, the consequences may be fatal."[52]

Sometimes, it's hard to stand by and watch our children suffer the unpleasant consequences of their choices. We love them and want to protect them. But protecting them is not always the most loving thing a parent can do.

177

Learning the Hard Way

In the biblical story known as the "Prodigal Son,"[53] there's no doubt that the father dearly loved his two sons. One day, the youngest asked his father for his share of the family inheritance. He didn't want to wait until his father's death. He wanted to enjoy his share now.

Later events in the story make clear that the son was still very immature, and his father surely realized it. He probably foresaw much of the foolish behavior in which his son later engaged and which resulted in his wasting his inheritance. I'm sure that the father advised his son to reconsider his decision.

In the end, however, the father honored his son's choice. He let him go off on his own and waste his inheritance on what the story describes as "riotous living." Penniless, the son had to take a job feeding pigs just to survive. He was so hungry, he wished he could eat even as well as the pigs. Ashamed of his foolishness, he returned home to beg his father to hire him as a servant. That way, he could once again enjoy at least a small bit of comfort and security. He had learned his lesson the "hard way."

When he was fourteen, I stopped telling my son when to go to bed. I didn't make a big deal of it. I just stopped reminding him that it was time for bed. At first, he stayed up too late a few times. But he didn't like being sleepy and irritable in school the next day, so he began to go to bed at about the same time I would have set for him, sometimes even earlier. But I didn't have to set or enforce his bedtime. He chose it. He had made some poor choices about bedtime, suffered the consequences and learned from his (ultimately harmless) mistakes. Learning that way was much more effective than if I had simply nagged him. And I didn't have to!

That's another benefit of letting children experience the consequences of their actions. Often, they discover their own limits (how much sleep they need, how much time it takes to finish their chores) and then "self-correct," choosing their own appropriate limits. That's very "adult" behavior and a good one for any child to learn![54]

But what if they don't "self-correct"? What would I have done if my son had gone for two weeks staying up until midnight, repeatedly falling asleep in school and perhaps even getting sick from being over-tired? Then, it's time to **temporarily** take back the choice that was given. "You're falling asleep in school and getting sick from being over-tired. I can see that you're not getting enough sleep. Please be in bed by 10:00 P.M. from now on." Then, after some appropriate time for your child to learn (perhaps six months or a year), you let them try again. Highly successful parents understand that, in the end, a child needs to learn to make good choices and gain confidence in their ability to make them. That can only come with practice (and successes and failures).

An Ancient Idea

The idea of letting people learn by making choices and experiencing the consequences is really nothing new. In fact, it's quite ancient. Not only is it illustrated by the story of the Prodigal Son, but is also found in the way God dealt with his people in Biblical times.

In the biblical book of the Exodus, chapters 20-23, God gives His people a series of rules (most notably, the Ten Commandments) to govern their living. The people were responsible for choosing whether to obey or not, but if they didn't obey, they had to live with the consequences. Nevertheless, the rules and the consequences clearly had a very positive, redemptive purpose: to train them in right living as his people. For that reason, they were always given and applied within the context of God's unconditional love and forgiving grace toward his people.[55] He always let them choose. He never stopped loving or forgiving them.

179

Following God's lead, highly successful parents are convinced that the discipline of their children involves loving and gracious discipleship; a partnership that helps children grow into greater and greater responsibility for their behavior. Children are given greater choices appropriate to their age and are enabled to learn from the results of their choices with less nagging, punishment, friction and power struggles.

This positive approach to discipline also encourages children to live up to their parents' standards. When they fail, they are held accountable. Since, however, the parents' goal is not primarily to "catch 'em doing wrong and punish 'em" but to help them learn to do better the next time, children who fail experience a balance of firmness and accountability with kindness and forgiveness from their parents. They know their parents are "on their side," helping them to turn failure into an opportunity to learn.[56]

I know from experience that this approach to discipline is a lot of work! It takes more thinking, more planning, and more self-control than just "doing what comes naturally." But successful parents know that, in the long run, it pays much greater returns in the lives of our children. They're convinced that, in developing self-discipline, "practice makes perfect!"

7. Keep the Faith , your sense of humor, and a sense of perspective!

I grew up in a family of four children, each two to three years apart. We were just close enough in age to be textbook examples of "sibling rivalry"—always fighting over something small, but important to us. At least four times an hour, it seemed, one of us would run to Mom to complain of some terrible injustice perpetrated on us by a sibling. "Don't make a federal case out of it," she'd say. That was her way of telling us to relax and keep things in perspective. Every problem isn't major. Some things can be treated with the neglect they deserve.

180

Highly successful parents know that, too! Every little failure isn't worth nagging or rebuking a child for. There are those times when it won't make a whole lot of difference if things aren't done "just right, right now" whether it's taking out the garbage or cleaning up a room.

Children have bad days and bad moods, just like the rest of us. Sometimes they, like us, "do what they want instead of what they should." So Dr. Penelope Leach has some common sense advice for us. "Choosing to ignore unimportant things—especially sulky faces or tones of voice—keeps the atmosphere more pleasant, gives your children space for private feelings and relationships, and saves your thunder for things that really matter."[57]

To help us save our "parental thunder" for the really important things, my wife and I try to live by *The DSSS Rule: "Don't Sweat The Small Stuff."* Since much family strife in our house really is over things that aren't important in the long run, here's an important corollary to the DSSS Rule: *"Remember: Most Things are Small Stuff!"* Highly successful parents keep those two rules in mind to help them avoid making "a federal case out of everything" when their children are less than perfect (much of the time)!

And sometimes, when your children have been far less than perfect, a little humor can be just what is needed. Laugh a little. Have a funny saying in your family that can trigger a smile or chuckle when one is desperately needed. When your child whines or complains, try, "I guess it's just a bad day. I think I'll whine, too!" Both you and your child may end up dissolved in laughter!

When all is said and done, there are no guarantees in life; either that children will have perfect parents or that parents will raise children who become perfect adults. We do our best for eighteen years or so, and then our children grow up and move away. They become independent adults. That's what we've worked for. That's God's plan.

As adults, our children make their own choices. Some are good; some are not. But they are our children's choices, not ours. That, too, is God's plan. In the end, there are no guarantees except one. God is faithful. We can trust him. He honors our efforts to be the best parents we can be. When our children are grown and leave home, we may be done with our parenting, but God is not. Long after our children have left our home, He hears our prayers for them. Long after we are no longer there for our children, He is. All that we've taught them of God's love, forgiveness, and standards will remain with them. He loves our children even more than we do.

Highly successful parents trust God. They know he is faithful. They know they can trust their children to him. They may fail, but God never will.

Chapter 8

Spanking and Its Alternatives

There's no doubt about it. Whenever parents discuss methods of discipline, spanking is always on the list. One psychologist said, almost all parents today see spanking as "an inevitable part of raising children."[1] Inevitable or not, it's a controversial one!

Spanking has been a discipline tool of American parents for generations. A recent survey showed that 76% of those questioned said that "spanking was an effective form of discipline in their homes when they were children."[2] So, it's no surprise that "the vast majority of people today still believe it's OK for parents to spank their kids."[3]

I was spanked as a child and I think I turned out okay. Maybe the same applies to you. Still, I'm going to caution you against taking "spare the rod, spoil the child" literally. Highly successful parents have come to understand that there are some very good reasons to think carefully before taking that bit of advice as the basis for disciplining (and discipling) their children.

"Spare the rod, spoil the child" is an oft-quoted piece of commonly held parenting advice. Many parents, (especially Christian parents) often assume the phrase is a direct quotation from the Bible. In fact, although there are references to "the rod' and "the child," the words "spare the rod, spoil the child" are themselves nowhere to be found in the Bible.   The phrase itself was probably invented by someone to explain and justify spanking based on biblical references such as these from the book of Proverbs: "He who spares the rod, hates his son, but he who loves him is careful to discipline him;"[4] "Do not withhold punishment from a child. If you punish him with the rod, he will not die;"[5] and "Folly is bound up in the heart of a child, but the rod of discipline will drive it far from him."[6]

What do you suppose the word "rod" meant to the writer of these Proverbs? In the context of biblical times, it could have had a number of meanings. Parenting writer John Rosemond helpfully points out that the rod is "a traditional and ancient measure of length and as such means that parents should define the limits for their children."[7] Rosemond asks what kind of "rod" can a child be beaten with and stand absolutely no chance of dying (as one of the proverbs above says)? He observes that the same word used for "rod" in this Proverb is used in Exodus 21:20 to refer to a man beating his slave with a rod so that the slave dies. If the slave died, why not the child? Perhaps, Rosemond says, the "rod" of Proverbs is a metaphor for steadfast, firm and consistent discipline, and not a stick at all.[8]

In support of that theory, Rosemond notes that the Hebrew word for "rod" used in Proverbs is also used in the book of Isaiah "to suggest a relatively flimsy instrument used to thresh caraway *so as not to damage it*" (his emphasis).[9] The writer says that caraway is beaten with a rod, yet he makes the point that the process is relatively gentle. Since threshing is the process of separating the grain from the chaff, perhaps the rod here is a metaphor for discipline as a process of separating useful behaviors from those that aren't.[10]

This relatively gentle understanding of the rod squares with that of Jack and Judith Baliswick, parents and seminary professors. They write that the rod used in the agricultural and pastoral context of biblical times "was an instrument to guide ignorant sheep, not a means of beating them into submission."[11]   It is also revealing to note, as Rosemond does, that Proverbs 22:6, the most famous of all Bible verses on child-rearing, "Train a child in the way he should go and when he is old he will not turn from it,"[12] doesn't mention the rod at all.[13]

Although the Bible does use many metaphors throughout its pages, it is possible that the rod may be some literal sort of instrument of punishment. If so, it would seem that this rod was not to be used for frequent, harsh beatings but relatively sparingly and gently for correction. Regardless, we can conclude at least this: parents were directed to discipline, that is train, their children through firm, consistent, and loving actions which may occasionally include the careful, sparing use of spanking.

Using This Tool Properly

Is "spare the rod, spoil the child" just another way to say spanking is good and more spanking is better? Parents disagree. Some successful parents choose not to spank at all. For other, equally successful parents (perhaps the majority) spanking is a discipline option.   But they agree with the experts that, to be effective, spanking must be used with great caution.

Why such concern for caution? Because spanking, like any tool in a workers toolbox, can do damage if not used properly. Here are some guidelines that highly successful parents follow to assure the proper, effective and careful use of spanking.

1. Spank as discipline not punishment.

Highly successful parents use spanking as a tool, not a weapon (parents don't use weapons on their children). It is a tool to get a child's attention so that you can use other methods to correct their behavior or to help your child regain self-control.

Some parents often use spanking as punishment. But, as we've already seen, punishment isn't discipline. The two are quite different. Discipline is "a system of giving positive guidance to children"[14] It sets limits, corrects wrong behavior, demonstrates right behavior and leads a child to want to do better the next time. It is based on a discipling relationship of mutual love and respect. As one insightful doctor put it, " a spanking should always be motivated by love for the purpose of teaching and correcting, never for revenge," or I might add, simply expressing anger or causing pain.[15]

Punishment, in contrast, is essentially negative. Its purpose is to hurt. Spanking used as punishment may reduce misbehavior but doesn't correct it. "In this sense" says John Rosemond, "a spanking is an extremely ineffective consequence" of wrong behavior. Parents who think otherwise "cannot understand why, no matter how often or how hard they spank, the misdeeds in question keep occurring."[16] Spankings are largely ineffective in teaching correct behavior and therefore in teaching children much that's useful about life in general.

Just what is spanking, anyway? Is it done with one's hand or another object? Is it done only a certain number of times or until a certain effect is attained? I like John Rosemond's definition: "a swat (or perhaps two) swiftly applied to a child's rear end by means of a parent's open hand. The purpose is **not** to cause pain, but to (a) secure the child's immediate, undivided attention; (b) quickly terminate an undesirable behavior; (c) secure control of a situation that threatens to quickly deteriorate; (d) provide a forceful reminder of your authority; or (e) all of the above. In other words, a spanking is nothing more than an occasionally effective form of nonverbal communication."[17]

Rosemond's definition of spanking illustrates spanking used as a tool of discipline; to help you stop undesirable behavior, get control of the situation, and get your child's attention so that you can follow up with instructive and corrective consequences and direction. Since the purpose is not punishment or pain, usually a swat (or two at the most) is all that is necessary. For Rosemond, spankings have a positive, restorative goal of helping the child regain self-control. And self-control is, after all, the ultimate goal of discipline.

Spanking can seriously interfere with discipling and discipline, especially if the child is above the age of six. I learned that first hand in attempting to "discipline" my seven year-old foster daughter. When a child is determined not to cry or not to change his behavior and you're just as determined that he will, spanking can actually increase a child's defiance. Some children react to force "by becoming so defiant that they will endure tremendous pain rather than obey."[18] When that happens, spankings may escalate in frequency and intensity and create tension and power struggles in the family that make discipling (giving positive guidance to children) impossible.

That said, we can state that, used appropriately as discipline rather than punishment, a swift swat or two (what Rosemond calls a "potch en tuckus;" a Yiddish phrase meaning a light spanking to the rear)[19] can be a very useful parental tool.

2. Spank sparingly.

Unfortunately, some adults who were frequently spanked as children still carry strong feelings of resentment about it. If they talked too loudly, they were spanked. If the spilled their milk at dinner, they were spanked. If they teased their siblings, they were spanked. Their resentment and anger (much of it justified) made it impossible for them to hear and accept the many good things that their parents wanted to teach them.

Highly successful parents know that spanking is subject to the "law of diminishing returns." The more you use it, the less effective it becomes. So they use it sparingly and only for blatantly disrespectful, flagrantly disobedient, outspokenly defiant, extremely rude, or insensitive behavior.[20] When they do spank, they save it for major problems, such as rebellion, defiance, and dangerous behavior. Spanking for minor problems, such as those related to childishness and immaturity, for example, doesn't make a lot of sense. Children do act childish and immature because they're children. Understanding that is basic to treating them with the respect they deserve. Time will cure much of their impatience, stubbornness, selfishness, and clumsiness. Spanking for such instances doesn't help. And successful parents know they can likely help their children learn to act better with other, more effective kinds of discipline.

Highly successful parents generally regard spanking as a "last resort." They use less drastic forms of discipline "such as verbal correction, timeout and logical consequences" first. If these fail, then spanking may be necessary.[21] Successful parents know that, when used infrequently, spanking can be just the surprise needed to shock a child out of his undesirable actions or attitude. But if used for every little offense, spanking loses much of its effectiveness as a tool of discipline. And if overused, spanking is seen by the child as unfair and undeserved. It can foster a bitterness and resentment that cuts off the possibility of discipling.

When successful parents do spank, they try to be sure their child understands (as much as possible) why he or she was spanked. This is important to the corrective, restorative aspect of discipline. And, if a child understands the reason for being spanked, he's less likely to feel resentful.[22]

Of course, it may occasionally be necessary to swat two to four years olds who are too young to understand the reasons behind your safety rules ("don't run in the street," "stay away from the stove"). A swat or two to the rear now and then may literally keep them safe enough to grow up! But even four and fives may have a hard time learning much from a spank. The urge to explore is strong! And spanking teaches only a "Don't" not a "Do." With a child of that age, it might be wiser to carefully teach them basic safety rules, such as looking both ways before crossing the street, and to require them to be supervised when going into or across the street until they prove they've learned the rules![23]

Highly successful parents save spanking for when it's really needed. As one expert wisely observed, "Using spanking for minor problems is like using a chainsaw to build a picture frame. It may work, but you'll probably do more than you wanted to, and frequently it won't fit together like you intended it to."[24]

3. Spank quickly.

Spanking as discipline is only effective if used to get your child's attention and get control of a situation before it's too late. So if you need to administer a swat or two to stop a behavior, do it immediately!

Successful parents don't waste a lot of time threatening or talking. If the situation warrants a spank, it warrants it now. If you wait until you are "at the end of your rope" and you can't take it any longer, you're likely to be so angry and frustrated that you'll take it out on your child with an overly harsh spanking. Then, you feel guilty and your child feels resentful. Nothing good was accomplished.[25]

Guideline #2 still applies; *Spank Sparingly.* But when a spank is warranted, successful parents do it right then. They don't wait "until Dad or Mom gets home." They address the situation. That way, correction and learning can take place. The reason for spanking is to assert your authority and get control of this situation immediately—to get the child's attention and help them regain self control **now**.

I realize that many experts advise never spanking in anger. That's good advice if you're using spanking as punishment and intend to really wallop your child. Then you run the very real risk of abuse. But if you're spanking as discipline (intending to administer 1-2 swats for the clearly defined purposes we've discussed), you needn't wait until you're not angry. It's alright to be angry as long as you're not out of control. Children need to realize their improper behavior can make us angry. If you spank quickly, at the beginning of a serious situation, you're less likely to be out of control. As long as you're in control, spank when necessary—even if you're angry.

4. Limit spanking to certain ages.

What about spanking babies and toddlers? Respected Parenting Specialist and writer Dr. Kay Kuzma says simply, "Spanking babies is abusive." She says babies misbehave largely out of frustration or simply because they don't know any better. "Prevention is the best answer. If you can meet the needs of the baby before they get frustrated and out of control, you can avoid many misbehavior problems. But even if you can't prevent a problem, spanking isn't the answer."[26] She recommends holding tight and close a baby having a tantrum until they relax. If the baby is getting into something, divert their attention. Babies are wonderfully easy to distract!

Highly successful parents understand that spanking babies and toddlers is abusive because it achieves nothing good and plenty of harm. Below the age of two, a child is unable to understand why he is being spanked (for not staying still on the changing table or spilling his food off his tray). He is just too young to make the connection between what he did and the swat he received. Spanking does little, if any, good and just confuses him about why someone he loves is hitting and hurting him!

One of the most common uses of spanking is to keep your toddler from pulling things off your favorite shelf and breaking them or playing with your make-up in the bathroom. Again, spanking does little to solve the problem. Dr. William Sears, the well known Christian pediatrician, observes that, even if a toddler is spanked "on the spot, there's no real guarantee he'll remember the lesson the next time." Instead of spanking, "the parents' job of discipline consists primarily of supervising the child so as to keep her away from possible harm."[27] This is what we called "child-proofing" the house when our boys were young; making their environment safe for them to explore and still keeping us sane!

A good rule to follow is this one developed by a doctor and published in Dr. James Dobson's "Focus on the Family" magazine: "Spanking is inappropriate before 15 months old and is usually not necessary until after 18 months. It should be less necessary after 6 years and rarely, if ever, used after 10 years of age."[28]

We did spank our sons when they were preschool age, but I don't believe we ever spanked them beyond the age of six or seven. After that, anything more than an occasional single swat to get attention probably causes too much humiliation and resentment to be effective in any way. Successful parents know that, with children above the age of six or seven, there are more effective ways to correct wrong behavior and, at the same time, to teach what is right.

5. Limit spanking to a few swats.

How many spanks should I administer to my child? The answer lies in whether you're using spanking as discipline or punishment. If your purpose is discipline, one or two appropriate swats to the child's posterior will be sufficient to get his attention, assert your authority and help him regain his self-control. If you spank sparingly, the surprise factor, together with the child's realization that this must be a major infraction, will add impact to your swat.

Never give more than three swats! It's simply not necessary when using spanking as a tool of discipline (rather than punishment) and it will help prevent unintentional abuse. Highly successful parents know that spanking "should leave only a transient redness of the skin and never cause physical injury."[29] Anything more is abuse.

6. Spank in Private.

Some of us have distinctly unpleasant memories of being spanked with other adults (and even worse, our siblings!) standing there gawking. It was a humiliating experience—sometimes even worse than the spanking itself. Since the purpose of discipline is discipleship, teaching, and correction, intentional and avoidable humiliation is totally inappropriate. So highly successful parents spank in private whenever possible.

If you're dealing with a toddler for whom a "potch en tuckus" may save her from the danger of a busy street or a hot stove, a swat in private may not be possible. But in most other cases, it will be. If you're visiting a friend or neighbor, they've probably got a bedroom or bathroom that would serve the purpose. Even malls and public buildings have alcoves and other places where a swift swat or two can be administered with a little privacy. Highly successful parents are convinced that spanking in private is parenting by the Golden Rule. It shows their respect for the dignity and feelings of their child. They know the purpose of the spank is corrective and restorative, not to humiliate.

7. Be careful to follow-through.

I took golf lessons once, but I just couldn't keep the ball on the fairway. I even tried tennis, but that was a disaster for me. I don't claim to know much about either game, but I did learn one thing about playing successfully: Hitting the ball is only the beginning. The follow-through is just as important.

After a swat or two has caught a child's attention and helped them regain control of the situation, successful parents know it's time for the follow-through. That's the "consequence," Rosemond says. Without a proper consequence, the spanking is "inconsequential." It's intended to stop undesirable behavior and get control of the situation but not to teach or correct. So an immediate consequence is needed to complete the job.

A consequence may be a stern reprimand, a loss of privileges, or a time out (we'll talk more about consequences shortly). The important thing, Rosemond says, "is that the spanking not be the consequence, the end in itself. When spankings are administered as if they were an end in and of themselves, parents tend, out of frustration, to overuse them and edge ever closer to abuse."[30]

But highly successful parents are convinced that there is one more essential element of follow-through. After the spank, they hug their child, remind them that they are greatly loved, and re-establish the relationship.[31] These parents are not upset if the child is angry or not ready to be "warm and cuddly" after a spank, but they do want to remind their child of the bigger picture of their love and care for the child. Highly successful parents know that they can never give their child too much assurance of their love. And they understand that *spanking, like all corrective measures, is most effective if "used only when the child receives at least as much encouragement and praise for good behavior as correction for problem behavior."*[32]

8. <u>Spank with common sense.</u>

The biggest questions many parents ask about spanking is, "When? When do I spank, and when do I employ some other tool?" There are no formulas to follow. You have to use your best judgement and what we've called "sanctified common sense." When your kids are fighting and driving you nuts, spanking may stop it temporarily. But what about the long run goal of discipline: learning for life? Telling them "if you can't play nicely together, you'll need to play apart" may be just as effective at stopping the squabbling and forces them to work at learning to settle their disputes on their own.

When your preschooler draws on the wallpaper, the urge to spank to make your point unmistakably can be almost irresistible. But remember, your child may not understand "why you complimented her on her pretty drawing yesterday but are furious today". So highly successful parents may explain the difference between paper and walls and clean up together—at least the first time![33]

Some parents spank when their child hits a playmate ("I want him to know how it feels") or takes away a playmate's toy forcibly. It's just as effective to set up a non-negotiable rule that "hitting is not allowed in our house" and having a consequence such as a timeout or ending the play date. An approach that is centered on discipline rather than punishment will seek to know what prompted the hitting. Was your child frustrated by something her playmate did? If so, it's important to teach your child that she should express her frustration with her words, not her hands! Similarly, if your child wants to play with another child's toy, you need to train him to ask first, not to just grab. That's discipline in the sense that we've understood it. "Use your words!" may be your refrain for some time, but the message will get through!

Highly successful parents do spank but not for minor offenses, not frequently, and not very young children or children above age six or seven. But given those guidelines, when they think a spank is called for, they do it. They trust their own judgement and their sanctified common sense.

A Note of Caution!

Throughout our discussion of spanking, I've used John Rosemond's definition of the term: a strictly limited number of swats (1-3) to the bottom for the purpose of furthering a child's self-discipline. I think you can see that I recommend against using spanking as punishment, to inflict pain. If you decide to do so, however, the above guidelines aren't enough.

If you spank as punishment, many times one or two swats won't be enough to inflict the pain and discomfort you intend. If that's the case, forget what I said about spanking when angry and spanking quickly. There's too much risk of your spanking escalating into abuse. Better to observe these two rules: *Pray First* and *Never Spank in Anger or When You Feel Out of Control.* Successful parents understand that spanking is much more effective as a planned reaction to misbehavior than as an angry outburst. Praying will help you calm down and put the situation in perspective. Then, when your anger has cooled, you're ready to proceed.

And good follow-through is even more important: be sure to "make up" afterward. Allow your child to be sad; even angry at you for awhile. That's a normal reaction that you'd have in the same situation. But then, go into the room and offer a hug, a story, time on your lap, and assurance that "I love you." Young children need to experience reconciliation with you after a misdeed, just as we desire that same reconciliation and assurance of God's continuing love for us!

What about the claims of many "experts" that spanking warps children emotionally and teaches them to solve their problems with violence? Most parents today— even those who don't spank their children—know those claims fly in the face of both common sense and experience. Surveys show that about four out of five adults say they were spanked as children.[34] "Everyone I know was taken to the woodshed every now and then," said one mother. "And I don't see anyone harboring any great emotional anxiety because of it."[35]

Highly successful parents are well aware that "there is absolutely no worthwhile evidence to support the notion that children who are occasionally (the operative word) spanked stop trusting their parents and begin fearing them instead; no reason to believe that parents who spank are certain to do so more often and more severely over time; nothing but thin air supporting the claim that spankings induct children into a 'culture of violence'; nothing but rhetoric behind the notion that spankings *per se* engender psychological problems." These claims are nothing more than inventions and myths.[36]

Some successful parents are not ready to agree with the many experts (from both conservative and liberal camps) who say parents should never spank. These parents feel that spanking is not essential to successful parenting and is far from the ideal method of controlling and shaping their children's behavior. Nonetheless, they see no evidence that a mild spanking is harmful to children.   And "indeed, spanking is supported by history, research and a majority of primary care physicians."[37]   Yet, successful parents know that there are other creative and effective methods of discipline at their disposal. Let's discuss some of them now.

Truth or Consequences?

"Sometimes the best way to discipline is to do nothing at all," says Dr. Mitch Golant. No, he's not another crazy, impractical "expert."   He and his wife, Susan, advocate teaching children self-discipline by use of natural and logical consequences.

If your child refuses to eat at mealtime, just remove his plate. It's a good bet that before the next meal, "his body will soon tell him the consequence—hunger. The next time he will be more responsible for his eating. Thus, you avoid always having to exert control, while he learns from his choices."[38] This is an illustration of letting a child learn from the "natural consequences" of their choices. If the child doesn't eat when food is available, it follows naturally that they'll be hungry. It isn't something imposed on her by her parents; it's just a natural consequence of her own choice. And since she made the choice and the resulting consequence wasn't imposed as punishment, the child often learns quicker and easier.

Being tired the next day when you stay up too late and don't get enough sleep or being hungry when you don't eat are natural consequences of those actions. They're called "natural" consequences because they're going to happen "naturally," whether you or I as parents do anything or not. In his book *Children: The Challenge,*[39] Rudolf Dreikurs is widely credited with developing the idea of natural and logical consequences as a means of helping children develop good self-discipline. To determine the "natural consequences" of a child's action, just ask yourself "What will happen naturally if I don't intervene?" That's the likely natural consequence.

Dreikurs tells the story of ten year-old Alfred, who was always forgetting to take his lunch to school and calling his mother to bring it to him (you can tell Dreikurs wrote in the '60's, before the era of many mothers working outside the home!). She quickly grew tired of that and decided to let him experience the "natural consequence" of forgetting his lunch: being hungry. Alfred didn't like being hungry all afternoon so it wasn't long before he became very good at remembering to take his lunch![40]

How would Dreikurs deal with a four year-old who dawdles over her food and refuses to eat despite the many entreaties of her parents? After the meal is over, remove the unfinished food and allow the natural consequences to do their work, he suggests. Since no food is available to her until the next meal, the child will soon learn that if you don't eat when food is available, you get hungry. Sure, she'll be uncomfortable, but not as uncomfortable as if she were spanked or nagged throughout the meal (and her parents can enjoy the meal a lot more, too!). No lasting harm is done by the natural consequences, and a lasting lesson will be learned.[41]

Regarding natural consequences, you may also want to ask "Will they be harmful?" A temporary experience of hunger between meals may be unpleasant, but won't harm a child. It may, however, solve a problem and teach an important lesson. Being tired (even falling asleep) in school one or two days will not do any long term harm to a child, and it may teach a lesson about the importance of reasonable bedtimes. On the other hand, if your three year-old keeps running out of the yard into the busy street or your teen is experimenting with drugs, the natural consequences can be deadly. In other situations, such as not getting homework done on time or failing to take out the trash before the weekly neighborhood pick-up, there simply are no "natural" consequences to help children learn. In those cases, something else is needed.

Doing What Comes Logically

When there are no natural consequences to a certain action or they are dangerous or impractical, the highly successful parent establishes certain consequences that follow from the child's action and which are related to them logically enough to help teach a life lesson. Dreikurs called these "logical" consequences because they are set up to follow logically after certain behaviors. In that way, they, too, teach important life lessons.[42]

You can't allow your three year-old to experience the natural consequences of running into the street, so you set up logical ones. "You can either play in the yard and not go in the street, or, if that's too hard, you can play indoors." Then, she will indicate her choice by her behavior! If her choice is to play indoors, that's fine. She will learn that if she wants to play outdoors, she must stay in the yard.

Successful parents of teens find logical consequences to be especially helpful. For example, if you don't put your clothes in the wash, what happens? They aren't washed and ready to wear when you want them. If you don't get up and get ready for school when the alarm clock rings, so that you miss the bus, you may walk (or, if that's not possible, you perform one of the parents weekly chores to repay them for the time spent taking you to school) or experience the discomfort and inconvenience of being late. If you violate your curfew, you pay a "fine" of double the amount of time of your violation and come in that much earlier the next time.

Did you notice that, in talking about discipline, we've not used the word "punishment"? Having to walk to school if you miss the bus, pay a fine for a curfew violation, or go hungry if you don't eat at mealtime, could all be considered punishments. In some cases, they look pretty much the same as punishment might look. But there is a difference. Highly successful parents know that it's not so much what you do but how you do it!

Telling your child "You'd better eat that right now or go hungry the rest of the night" is a threat. Enforcing it feels like punishment to the child. We don't like to admit it, but sometimes the purpose of punishment is to "show them who's boss" or get back at their negative behavior. When that's the case, punishment makes the child feel angry, resentful and even rebellious ("I'll show them!") and revengeful ("I'll get even!"), instead of thinking about their responsibility for their actions and what they should be learning from the consequences.[43]

Avoid "I Told You So!"

Successful parents try to avoid threats, anger and scolding whenever possible. As calmly, clearly, and pleasantly as they are able, they let their child know the consequences and then let them choose. "It's our rule here that if you don't eat at meal time, you can't eat snacks, and I'm afraid if you don't eat your dinner, you'll be awfully hungry later. Is that okay?" Then, after dinner, when your child complains of being hungry, you won't say "I told you so," but "I'll bet you are. And I'm sorry, but you'll be alright until breakfast. There'll be more to eat then."

When your three year-old runs into the street instead of staying in the yard, it's easy to yell angrily "I told you to stay in the yard. Now, you come in here and stay in here for the rest of the day!" That sounds like punishment to your child. Although it's harder, successful parents try to calmly say something like, "I'm sorry it was too hard for you to stay in the yard, but the street is too dangerous. You'll have to play inside for the rest of today and then you can try the yard again tomorrow. I know you'll do better then."

Notice that the actual consequence was exactly the same: playing inside for the rest of the day. But which situation do you think was easier for the child to learn a life lesson from? In the first, both parent and child were no doubt angry and frustrated. The second did not cast the situation as a power struggle between the parent's rules and the child's will, but as an attempt by the two of them together to help the child develop the self-discipline needed to play outside. There is an element of hope and encouragement for the child, also. They will get another chance (aren't we all thankful for more chances?) and will likely do better. That's discipline in its true, most positive sense.

It's not easy! I know—I've tried it! But it really is a better way! After all, successful parents don't want to always be in power struggles with their children. They want to be "pulling together" with their children; to let them know they're on the same side as they work together toward their growing maturity and responsibility. Letting children learn from the consequences of their actions while trying to keep a sympathetic attitude helps them learn those lessons more effectively. And both parent and child enjoy each other a whole lot more in the process!

Ultimately, *highly successful parents are convinced that children learn best through the consequences of their behavior*, especially if they realize that the rules are a product of their parents' love and concern for them. This is in contrast to training children "primarily by punishing their negative behavior, an approach which puts all the responsibility on the parents....It is more helpful for children to understand that their behavior has specific consequences and that the ultimate responsibility rests with them."[44] After all, that's the way it will be when they grow up. Most of life will be their responsibility.

Let the Consequences Fit

Sometimes, successful parents let their children and teens set the limits and consequences together with them. Family meetings can discuss the need for certain rules and behaviors and discuss and adopt appropriate consequences ("Everyone's weekly chores should be completed by noon on Saturday, or they pay a fine of double chores the following week"). That process just underlines who has the responsibility for certain behavior. Like most of us, children are more likely to obey rules and accept consequences that they've had a part in establishing.

"Let the punishment fit the crime" is an old common sense maxim that's a good guide for establishing consequences that teach children to be responsible while assuring them that they're loved. Highly successful parents believe that a consequence that teaches (as opposed to just punishing) should "fit" or be *related* to the action it follows. That way, it can teach a lesson about the results of that particular behavior.

In life, if you make a mess, you're responsible to clean it up. So if you play around at the dinner table and make a mess, you clean it up (and if the child is too young, perhaps they miss a favorite activity to pay back the time it took you to clean up after them). But going to bed without dinner or not going to play with a friend the next day is not directly related and doesn't teach the lesson effectively.

201

However, when a child is mean to a playmate, restricting her from inviting a playmate over for a day or two is related and should get the message across; "If you are unkind to people, no one will want to be your friend (or play with you)."

If your teen is on a quarterly clothing budget and spends all his money on two items of clothes the first week of the quarter, what happens when he "just has to have" something else three weeks later? In real life, if you exceed your budget, you either go without or find a way to earn extra money (you don't lose buying privileges for the next three years!). So those should probably be the same consequences facing your teen. They teach an important lesson for later in life. We need to try, fail, face the realistic consequences and then be able to try to do better the next time.

I hope you noticed that these consequences are not only related to the actions they follow, but they are also *reasonable*. No one learns much from being treated unreasonably except to be angry and resentful. If I get caught speeding, I expect to pay a fine. I'd consider it unreasonable to be sentenced to five years in jail! If your goal is teaching life lessons, as opposed to punishing, reasonable consequences are more effective.

So if your child forgets to feed the hamster and Mom or Dad does it, perhaps they pay a small fine or take over one of their parents chores. No TV for a week seems a bit unreasonable, doesn't it? If your teen comes in a half hour later than curfew, "grounding" for a week will likely seem so unreasonable as to block the learning of any lesson. But coming in an hour earlier the next night, while still a serious inconvenience, is not unreasonable.

There's one other important guideline for setting consequences. As much as possible, they ought to be *respectful* of the dignity of your child. Nothing loving or positive is accomplished by intentionally humiliating a child (though sometimes the natural consequences of their actions will do that). Slaps in the face and ridicule are never appropriate. When verbal rebukes or physical discipline are necessary, respect for the dignity of the child means taking them aside privately, if at all possible. Even in public places or someone else's home, there may be a bathroom or alcove where you can go. *Highly successful parents understand that it's hard to "disciple" someone while you are humiliating them.*

Those are the "3 Rs" of consequences: *"Related, Reasonable and Respectful"* [45] They're good guides for setting consequences that will help your children learn life-long lessons while assured of your equally enduring love!

There are also 3 "Cs" of successful discipline: *Calm, Consistent and Consequences.* "Calm discipline works more quickly and leads to less regrettable behavior" from both parent and child. [46] Correcting as calmly as you can helps you keep as positive an atmosphere as possible. Remember, you're ultimately engaged in discipling! Consistency is important, also. Successful parents are flexible enough to bend when the situation warrants, but their consistency helps their child to understand and accept the consequences (good or bad) of his actions. We've talked a lot about consequences because *highly successful parents are convinced that "consequences, not words, are the basic tools of discipline."* [47] Consequences are essential to teaching a child personal responsibility.

There's no doubt that it takes more thought and effort to discipline children through a system of natural and logical consequences than shouting and spanking. The best way isn't always the easiest. But in the end, successful parents know that the use of consequences is more effective in helping children develop into self-disciplined adults. And isn't that a major goal of our parenting?

Timeout!

Another popular discipline tool which successful parents use today is the "timeout." This usually means sending the child to a quiet corner, chair, or room for a specified period of time. Though the timeout was originally developed by psychologists to help them change the behavior of emotionally disturbed children, it "has gradually become popular with parents as a gentle alternative" to spanking.[48]

Timeout works because it deprives children of what they want the most: your attention or that of a friend or playmate. When a child misbehaves and loses your attention, that demonstrates to them very clearly "the basic truth that underlies all socialization: Unacceptable behavior spoils the interaction between people."[49] It results in some form of ostracism (prison is its most severe form) unless the undesirable behavior is changed.

Many successful parents have found timeout to be an effective alternative to spanking. And if you use it, you'll want to follow the same basic guidelines.

1. Use timeout as discipline, not punishment.

Timeout, as with a swat on the rear, is much more effective when used a tool of discipline, not as punishment. A timeout provides a break when a child is out of control; a chance for the child (and maybe you, too!) to calm down and regain self-control.

A timeout also breaks the chain of undesirable behaviors, defuses the situation, and provides an opportunity for a child to think about their choice of behavior and its consequences. That's what is needed for the child to establish or regain self-control. And that's the first step in developing self-discipline.

But when a timeout is over, highly successful parents instruct their child in a better choice of behaviors. Again, that is a major difference between discipline and punishment; the latter focuses most energy on punishing the bad behavior and neglects teaching the good. So timeout is most effective when used as "part of a well-planned system of discipline, one that emphasizes and rewards good behavior" as well as deterring undesirable actions.[50]

My wife uses timeout with the four and five year-olds in her public school preschool class. When the situation calls for it, children go sit in the "thinking chair." It's not a punishment as much as it is a chance to calm down and think about the consequences of their behavior and how they could do better the next time. In Sunday School, I've called it the "Opportunity Chair" (or corner) for the same reason.

You might also call time out "quiet time," signifying a few moments for the child to quiet down, get back in control, and get ready to do better. These are all positive names for the same tool. They point to the positive purpose behind the tool and put the responsibility for the use of that tool right where it belongs; on the child. If used this way, timeout can be a positive, restorative and effective tool to help your child develop self-discipline.

2. Use timeout sparingly.

This means reserving it for major problems, when they are really needed. One parent who uses timeout effectively recommends using it for hitting or biting, other ways of acting cruel to siblings or playmates such as name calling or excessive teasing, and for tantrums and major rebellious actions.[51]

Timeout can lose its effectiveness from overuse. Don't waste it on minor offenses like when the kids are noisy and you're tired, or they're fooling around at the table and spill their milk. Remember, it's an alternative to spanking. You'll use it in situations where you might otherwise have spanked, but not in any lesser ones.

3. Impose timeout quickly.

If you use it either as a consequence or as a way of interrupting and defusing a situation, impose it quickly. Don't let the situation get totally out of control. When your child does something serious such as hitting or biting, don't wait. Don't give a warning. You want to stop that behavior quickly. "The quicker you can draw a parallel between the cause (inappropriate behavior) and the effect (the consequence), the quicker your child will realize that some behaviors simply cannot be tolerated."[52]

4. Limit it to certain ages.

As we've seen, an effective timeout can a positive tool for teaching self-discipline to a child. But to benefit from it, children need to be able to understand what they did wrong and why they are going to a timeout. That's why Dr. Stephen J. Bavolek, Director of the Family Nurturing Center in Park City, Utah, recommends not using timeout before children are close to the age of four.[53] One of the real benefits of using the timeout is that, unlike spanking, it can be effective with children older than six or seven. Into the early teen years, a timeout may be just a child needs in order to settle down, think about what they're doing, and learn self-discipline.

5. Watch the clock.

How long should a timeout be? Long enough to achieve its purpose, but not too long. Because they're using timeout as a tool of discipline (not primarily to punish), highly successful parents want their child to successfully complete their time out with a minimum of struggle (Admittedly, that may take some practice!). As a child thinks about how to act better in the future and learns to gain control of their behavior, a timeout may become a somewhat positive experience for them. That's the way it should be!

When assigning a time out, successful parents watch the clock. They know what their child is capable of and assign the amount of time accordingly. If you have a very active five year-old who can't sit still for five minutes for **any** reason, a ten or fifteen minute timeout will probably just add to your troubles! They'll continually fail to "serve their sentence" and get more and more time added, until they've spent half the day in timeout and made both of you miserable, or until you give up and let them go.

The "one minute per year of age" rule is still a good one. But if your five year-old isn't capable of successfully completing a five minute timeout, start with 1-2 minutes. "The main thing," says Dr. Bavolek, "is that once your child has completed his timeout, he will feel successful and success is critical." If your child doesn't feel capable of meeting your expectation, the timeout will only increase their frustration, divert their attention from thinking about the situation they got themselves into, and make everything worse.[54] If they complete it successfully, a time out can be a positive experience that becomes a tool of self-discipline. Some successful parents even report children putting **themselves** in timeout when they know they need one!

6. Location, location, and location!

If you've ever bought or sold a house, you've heard the three factors real estate agents use in determining a fair market price for a house: "Location, Location, and Location." That's their way of saying how important location is to successfully selling a house.

Highly successful parents understand that location is important to a successful timeout, also. When we practiced timeout with our boys, we usually sent them to their room. Today, that may not be the best place. Many children have rooms today that look like self-contained entertainment centers. Featuring stereos, video games, even TV's, they're hardly places for quiet and reflection. And it does seem right that "a child's room should be a safe haven, a place of comfort and security," not a place associated with isolation, unpleasantness and punishment.[55]

The best location for an effective time out is some reasonably quiet place where the child can, indeed, settle down and think about the situation. That means a quiet, even boring place such as a corner or stairway. And whenever possible, successful parents choose a place where siblings won't be hanging around watching and adding to the child's embarrassment!

7. Remember to follow-through.

What happens at the end of a timeout is also critical to its success. When it is over, "let bygones be bygones." Don't welcome your child out of timeout by rehashing their problem and the lesson they learned. There'll be time to do that later. Discipline looks forward to doing better the next time, not backward to past failures. Your child has paid his debt. Now, he wants to get on with life. When a timeout is finished, Dr. Bavolek says, tell your child you appreciate his effort and cooperation. Then, take a walk, read a book or do "anything pleasant to show that after a quiet time out, life goes on."[56]

Highly successful parents are aware that even when a child has successfully completed a timeout, there's still danger of a "relapse." "The biggest mistake you can make is to let your child come out into exactly the same situation. He is certain to go back to the same behavior." So, after a time out, successful parents redirect their child into a new or more productive activity.[57] If he was pulling books off the shelves in the living room, get him interested in some rarely played-with toys in the family room. If she was fighting with a friend over a book, get them both interested in a game for two.

8. Use timeouts with common sense

Dr. Bavolek has some good, common sense advice for a successful timeout. You "want to be certain the child understands the purpose of the timeout so you might say something like 'You chose to break an important rule. The consequence is that you need a timeout to think about how you can do better the next time before you can play some more.'"[58]

Successful parents won't allow any discussion or talking during the timeout. It's meant to be a quiet time (some parents even call it that) and doesn't begin until the child is quiet. You may want to add a minute (a shorter period for young children) for violations. Some parents find it helpful to use a timer, also.

The key to success may well be what Dr. Bavolek calls, "time in." He explains that "timeout will never work unless the time in is positive." That means using timeout infrequently and as part of a "positive, structured form of discipline based on simple rules, praise, clear cut consequences and family cooperation."[59]

Successful parents apply that sound advice to the use of any tool of discipline. They don't overuse it. They do make it a small part of a larger system of clear, simple, positive rules and consequences, supported by lots of praise and encouragement, all within a loving family. Used that way, timeout can be an effective tool in preparing their children for life.

One Final Ingredient

We've talked about rules, consequences, consistency and firmness. They're all important to a successful program of discipline. Additionally, *highly successful parents are convinced that, ultimately, a program of discipline as discipling won't be successful unless it is grounded in love and one other important ingredient that we haven't discussed yet. It's one every successful parent uses: Mercy.*

Mercy is "letting someone off the hook"[60] because you love them. It's intentionally **not** giving the consequences a child's actions deserve. It's certainly a central (and much valued) feature of God's activity toward us. But is there a place for mercy in successful parenting? Some parents may fear that showing mercy to their children will undermine the value of consistency and thus weaken their children's growth in self-discipline. Of course, if mercy becomes an excuse for parental laziness—for consistently not holding children accountable for their behavior—it will have a negative effect.

Heather Harpham, in a helpful and insightful article called *Don't Forget the Mercy*, says that there are good reasons to show children mercy from time to time. Rather than undermining parental discipline, mercy may actually improve a child's willingness to accept and learn from it, she says. Many parents have had the experience of feeling truly guilty and sorry before God, not because they feared his punishment, but because they were keenly aware of his love and kindness. Our children may feel the same way toward us. We know that we parents "represent" God as heavenly parent to our children. Mercy is also a graphic illustration of what God is like. "When our children see that we are forgiving of their mistakes, they will have reason to believe that God will respond similarly," she says.[61]

One day when my oldest son was a preschooler, my wife got a $30 traffic ticket for parking in a "No Parking Zone." She had parked directly in front of a doctor's office on a busy city street during rush hour. She went to traffic court and pleaded for mercy. Yes, she was guilty, but our son was having a severe asthma attack and needed immediate medical attention. Her fine was forgiven. She received mercy.

We've all had experiences where we made a mistake, but mercy was warranted! Successful parents recognize that it happens with children, too. They also fall victim to "extenuating circumstances." Harpham notes how adults can talk about the terrible day they had at the office, the traffic jam on the way home, or whatever it was that made them crabby toward their spouse. Children may not be able to verbalize their crabbiness or frustration over a new toy that a playmate broke or their tiredness after being prematurely awakened from a nap, but they still need and deserve our mercy.

Common sense supports the use of mercy in discipline, also. No one benefits from being criticized and punished for each and every little failure to live up to the rules. That just produces discouraged and bitter children who eventually give up trying. The constant pain of failure is too great. *Highly successful parents are convinced that justice leavened with mercy produces a more palatable recipe for discipline.*

But how do you know when to show mercy and when not to show it? First, put yourself in your child's place. Remember any similar situation you experienced as a child. What did your parents do? How did it affect you? Sometimes, that's all it will take for you to know what to do. Harpham says mercy might be appropriate when you're so appalled by what your child did you can't think of a proper punishment. When you make a **big** mistake, that's when you would want and need mercy the most. And your child does, too. If it's an isolated incident, that might be a good time to show mercy. If you're dealing with a repeat problem or trying to break a bad habit, however, mercy may not be called for. A consistent follow-through with the promised consequences will be more helpful.[62]

Do you ever remember doing something you knew would upset your parents and feeling really, really sad about it? They didn't need to say anything. You felt terrible. No punishment could make you feel worse! If it is not a recurring problem and your child is truly sorry, it's a good time to show mercy. But successful parents make it clear that the next time, they'll have to follow-through with the consequences. And if a "next time" happens, they do. Of course, if the problem resulted from deliberate disobedience, mercy may not be appropriate, either.[63]

Successful parents know that "children will be children." They will be careless. They will be distracted. They will act like children. Even when the lamp is broken as a result of rough play or your clean rug shows dirty footprints, mercy may be called for. Just be sure they know that mercy is being applied, not that they are getting away with something. Let them know they're the object of mercy **this** time.

Mercy is the yeast that makes the bread of discipline "rise." As in making bread, you may use only a little, but it's one ingredient on which the entire recipe depends. So highly successful parents mix the daily discipline of their children carefully and lovingly with liberal amounts of mercy. They know that if they wait for their children to deserve mercy, they'll never give it. But they also know that mercy is rarely deserved by **anyone**! So they just give it anyway!

Chapter 9

God Isn't Finished

As we've traveled on our journey through the convictions of highly successful parents, I've shared with you lessons learned from twenty-five years of parenting, together with occasional "expert" opinions and a lot of "sanctified common sense" based on insights from God's Word. In essence, it all boils down to this. *Successful parenting will always be a challenge, even to the most hard working, spiritually and emotionally mature parent. But you can meet the challenge! By relying on your God-given good judgement and working hard to be the person God wants you to be, you can be a highly successful parent.*

Now, as we conclude our time together, permit me to summarize for you in the form of some practical "dos and don'ts" the convictions that guide highly successful parents. I've found this is a good way to remember these convictions.

First, here are what highly successful parents "don't."

1. They don't expect perfection.

They don't expect perfection, either from themselves or their children. Have you been to a college graduation lately? If so, you may have noticed that there were no college degrees awarded in parenting. No one received a

C.P.P. (Certified Perfect Parent) degree. Parenting is an art, not a science. Parents *do*, their children *become*. But in between our "doing" and their "becoming," there is room for an awful lot of mistakes! We will never earn that C.P.P. degree, but we will earn a H.S.P. (Highly Successful Parent) degree, and that's plenty good enough.

Highly successful parents understand that, like them, their children aren't perfect, either. After all, children are still apprenticing—learning how to live. Expecting them to be perfect only undermines their self-confidence and sets them up to see themselves as failures. Successful parents expect the best from their children (as well as from themselves), but not perfection. And since they don't expect it, their children don't disappoint them! So these parents are freed to love their children unreservedly and without disappointment.

2. They don't fear failure.
They don't fear occasional failures. Successful parents understand that mistakes are a normal and healthy part of parenting, so they aren't afraid of them. They make the best decisions that their sanctified common sense and good judgement allow, and when they're wrong, they learn from their mistakes and try to do better the next time. In this way, they add to their reserves of common sense and good judgement while protecting their self-confidence.

For successful parents, mistakes (by parents or children) are not failures, but opportunities to learn and do better. Without them, learning and growing isn't possible. So, successful parents don't fear mistakes, they welcome them.

3. They don't expect "smooth sailing."
They don't expect parenting to always be "smooth sailing." Our two sons are a delightful, unpredictable combination of both the physical and temperamental qualities of my wife and me. While that leaves no doubt that they're

214

our children, they're also very unique individuals. They've shown us again and again that children have their own (often inscrutable) opinions, preferences, and personalities. They make up their own minds and make their own choices, especially as they grow up. They aren't computers that can be programmed to turn out a certain way, no matter how hard we work or pray.

Inevitably, our children make choices that will make us say (hopefully under our breath!), "Where did **that** come from?" or "What were you thinking, if you were thinking at all?" More than once over the years from toddlers to teens, our responsibility to set limits and provide guidance to our children will clash with their desire to be independent and decide for themselves. Those clashes are inevitable. Successful parents aren't surprised or frightened by them. They expect them.

When those clashes come, our children will be unhappy, disappointed, or even angry with us, even for our most "right" decisions. The problem, as parenting expert John Rosemond says, is that many parents are "wimps" (as I was with my son that day in the doctor's office). They're convinced they should never say "No" to their children if it makes them unhappy.[1] Highly successful parents know that they must make the hard decisions as well as the easy ones. And some decisions will leave their children unhappy. But highly successful parents understand that their responsibility to their children is not always to please them or make them happy. It is, first of all, to be their parent, the one person they can count on to see the "big picture" that a child's eyes are too small to see and to make the hard decisions that are best for the child in the long run.

Children need parents who are willing to risk their child's anger to set healthy limits, while always balancing those limits with love. Children need parents who are firm and confident, yet kind and respectful, too; parents who live by the Golden Rule, so that their children learn to respect not only themselves, but their peers and parents as well.

4. They don't "go it alone."

They don't try to "go it alone." Being a highly successful parent means trusting yourself, but it doesn't mean being a "lone ranger." No one of us has the answer to every parenting challenge. But each of us has some of the answers, and together, all of us have all of the answers.

I've seen this demonstrated again and again in my parenting seminars. I've spoken to groups of parents from New York to Washington, D.C. and everywhere in-between. During the question and answer time there will always be questions that I don't have any idea how to answer (for example, questions about how to raise girls!). So I turn to my standard "expert" trick and say "Does anyone here have any experience with that?" Often, by the time the discussion is over, more than one person has offered a good and encouraging solution to the questioner's problem. Often, the solution is better than any I could have offered.

Highly successful parents are fully aware that they don't have all the answers, but they're convinced that, in most cases, somebody does. So they aren't reluctant to seek out the wisdom and experience of others. They may call up a trusted "grandma" or "grandpa," aunt or uncle (whether biological or honorary) for advice. They may have a cup of coffee with another mom or dad who is coping with, or already has successfully met, a challenge similar to theirs. Or they may turn to a "Mom's Day Out" or a "Promise Keepers" group. They know that, at the end of the day, the decision is theirs. Before they get there, however, there is plenty of wisdom waiting along the way to help them.

Every parent gets discouraged now and then. We all have doubts about our parenting. Why be embarrassed? Why pretend it isn't so? There are no special awards for parents who "go it alone." It's just a lot harder. Look for friends, neighbors, family, and fellow church members to share their common sense wisdom and give you a fresh perspective. They may have just what you—and your children—need!

Now, here are a few successful parenting "dos."

1. <u>They do try harder.</u>

Successful parents face the same time pressures we all battle: demanding jobs, children and spouses who need and deserve our time, financial challenges, you name it. So, they are also tempted to "shortcut" the time they give to parenting. But they know that a little time saved now may mean big losses in the future.

Here's how one insightful parent from Connecticut explained it: "The single most important thing I'd write in a parenting book—chapter one, page one, first paragraph, first sentence—is that you get back what you put in."[2]

That sounds like sanctified common sense to me! This parent has a clear sense of priorities. While balancing competing and conflicting job, personal, and family responsibilities, she is willing to put in the time and the effort required to give her children a sense of self-esteem, belonging and self-discipline. It isn't easy, but she's convinced that what she "puts in" now will determine what she "gets back" later. So she's willing to give a little more than the average parent, believing that, as a result, her children will be more than just "average" when they grow up!

Time with our children is, of course, one of the most important things that highly successful parents "put in" to their children. It provides the foundation for all the elements of family success.[3] But in addition to spending time with their children, highly *successful parents work hard at nurturing and developing themselves.*

It bears repeating once again: *"Good parenting begins with good personing."* The person you are determines the parent you are. You can't give your children more than you have. So successful parents work hard at growing in their own personhood, maturity, and integrity. They know that only by being the best person they can possibly be will they also be the best parent they can possibly be. They know their children will "take after them" in many ways. So they want to give their children a clear, consistent model of a mature adult to imitate.

As I've watched successful parents, I've observed that the most critical area in which successful parents work at personal growth is the spiritual. "Spirituality fosters parenting through example, the most durable parenting." Spirituality is also a " source of comfort, and strength, enabling parents to call on a unique authority for wisdom and direction."[4] That "unique authority" is, of course, God.

Highly successful parents are convinced that this spiritual principle applies directly to parenting: *As you deepen your personal relationship with God, you strengthen your parenting.* As you allow God to develop his own wonderful balance of love and limits, kindness and firmness, guidance and grace in you, you'll become a wiser, more mature, and gracious person—and therefore a much better parent, too.

That's why highly successful parents spend regular "quality time," not just with their children and spouses but with God; in personal study, prayer, small groups, and public worship services. They allow others to hold them accountable for this, even as they struggle with time pressures, job demands, and temptations of all kinds. Their spiritual growth may be slow, but it's also steady. And "slow and steady" is good enough to win the parenting race.

Enjoy Yourself!!

2. <u>They do enjoy being parents.</u>

Successful parents share the sentiments of the man who said "If I live to be 90, I want to be a dad all the way until I die."[5] They simply enjoy being parents. Not because it's easy or instantly rewarding but because of the great

218

privilege of sharing with God the joy and responsibility for shaping another unique and precious life.

When you care for two preschoolers, the days of diapers and babysitters seem like they'll never end. But as any parent of grown children will tell you, those days really do go by very quickly. So highly successful parents try to savor them. They want to enjoy their children! They immerse themselves in the exciting privilege of "apprenticing" or "discipling" their children. And the days truly do fly by. Soon, the pretty little girl in a frilly dress is a young woman off to college. Before you know it, the cute little guy helping you with the chores is borrowing the car!

As my sons have become young adults, I can imagine how Alice E. Chase felt when she wrote this poem, "To my Grown-up Sons." Her sentiments sound a bit quaint or "corny," but they'll ring true to the ears of any parent who has really enjoyed his or her children. They certainly do to mine.

> My hands were busy through the day,
> I didn't have much time to play
> the little games you asked me to.
> I didn't have much time for you.
>
> I'd wash your clothes, I'd sew and cook,
> but when you'd bring your picture book
> and ask me, please, to share your fun,
> I'd say "A little later, Son."
>
> I'd tuck you in all safe at night,
> and hear your prayers, turn out the light,
> then tiptoe softly to the door.
> I wish I'd stayed a minute more.
>
> For life is short and years rush past,
> a little boy grows up so fast.
> No longer is he at your side,

his precious secrets to confide.

The picture books are put away,
there are no children's games to play,
no good-night kiss, no prayers to hear.
That all belongs to yesteryear.

My hands, once busy, now lie still.
The days are long and hard to fill.
I wish I might go back and do
the little things you asked me to.[6]

Highly successful parents take time to enjoy their children. They make no apologies. They have no regrets. Of course, they **love** their children, but they *like* them and enjoy them, too! Spending time with their children is not just another duty or responsibility to be borne without complaint. They look forward to it.

Certainly, there are plenty of stressful times for parent and child alike. But successful parents know that times of stress and strain are normal and inevitable. So highly successful parents try, as much as possible, to "relax and enjoy the ride," bumps and all. They survive and thrive as parents by applying two of the most basic common sense rules of successful parenting: *Don't Sweat the Small Stuff* and *Remember that most things, after all, are Small Stuff.*

Trust God, Then Trust Yourself!

3. <u>They trust God and trust themselves.</u>

I'll never forget my embarrassment that day in the doctor's office when I had to be reminded that I, not my son, was "the parent." If I could live those moments over, that's one mistake I wouldn't make again! But a dozen years later, we've both survived! My son is a self-confident, well disciplined, splendid young man. And I did learn something

important from that incident.   I'm more self confident now.
I trust myself more as a parent.

But successful parents trust themselves precisely
because they, first of all, trust in God.   As Josh McDowell
says, "I know I don't have all the answers, but I know that
God does."[7] And He promises to give wisdom generously to
all who ask.[8]

So successful parents pray regularly (and ask others to
pray for them) for that wisdom God has promised.   Armed
with that gift, their decision making has the added advantage
of a "sanctified common sense" which helps them make even
the hardest decisions with calmness and confidence.   Highly
successful parents don't pretend to have all the answers, but
they know who does, and they ask him!

Highly successful parents never stop praying for
wisdom and never stop praying for their children, from their
child's birth until their own (the parent's) death.   *Highly
successful parents are convinced that praying is the best,
most effective thing they can do.*   Every day, as their
children pass through all the stages and dangers of life, they
commit them to the care of the father who loves their
children even more than they do!

God Isn't Finished

My oldest son is now completely independent and
living on his own.   His younger brother is starting college.
They're both sources of great joy and pride to their mother
and me.   And in just a few years, *both* will be on their own.
How will they "turn out"?   Will they become all that I've
hoped and prayed for them?   There are no guarantees.   Only
God knows.   And he's not finished with them yet.

When my son was ten and began to want all the latest
styles in (expensive!) sneakers and jeans, I feared I had
raised a confirmed materialist!   But then, he was only a child.
God wasn't finished with him yet.   And if my experience

with God's continual working in my middle-aged life is any clue, God won't be finished with my sons or me anytime soon. We all have a long way to "grow" before we "turn out."

While experience testifies that parents do tend to "get back" what they "put in," there are exceptions. Adam and Eve's son, Cain, was a murderer. Jesus told a story of a Prodigal son.[9] Ultimately, our children make their own choices. Sometimes, they do incredibly silly or foolish things, against our clear and forceful advice. Sometimes they make clearly destructive choices, against everything we've taught and modeled for them. "Train a child in the way he should go and when he is old he will not turn from it"[10] is not an iron-clad promise. It's a general principle of how God works through parents. Most of the time, our children do not turn from the way we've raised them. But not without exception. There are no guarantees, except that *God is faithful.*

In the end, every parent understands that there's no simple formula for raising the perfect offspring! No parent, gazing down at their beautiful newborn baby, knows how their child will turn out. Our children are beautiful, unfinished portraits being slowly and lovingly painted by God over the course of their entire lives. If you don't like everything you see in that portrait right now or if something isn't clear, don't worry. Keep trusting and praying. God isn't finished yet.

We may not see how our children will turn out because their story, like ours, won't be over until their lives are. God won't be finished with us until we meet him face to face. In the meantime, while we may not know if they'll turn out exactly as we hoped, we do know these two things: God asks us to be faithful in fulfilling his calling to us as parents and he, in turn, promises to be faithful to us.[11] We can trust in that faithfulness. It never fails.

And how thankful I am for that! Our children are also the recipients of the gracious and patient love of God, the God of second, third, and many more chances. Even highly successful parents don't always like what they see in their children at all times. But they never give up hope or stop praying. For as surely as the Prodigal Son wandered away, he also woke up to his folly and returned to his father's welcoming arms. Successful parents know that "the Lord will fulfill his purpose" for their children,[12] and it is a good purpose, to be sure! Only the Lord knows his plans for our children, but we know those plans are for good, not for harm, "to give [them] hope and a future."[13] Those are his promises. God is faithful. We can trust him.

So perhaps parents shouldn't be judged as successful or not by how their children "turn out," but rather by what they as parents, "put in." Successful parents will look back over their active parenting years and know that, while they weren't perfect, they were certainly "very adequate parents." They didn't do everything right all of the time but they *were* able to offer their children a loving, clear, and attractive example to follow most of the time. That's the ultimate measure of successful parenting—being faithful to our calling as parents, and trusting the results of our efforts to the faithfulness of God.

In this faithfulness and trust, and by living out the fundamental convictions in this book, I'm convinced that you will be a confident, highly successful parent. So why hesitate? Whether you're just beginning, midway through, or nearly finished with your active parenting journey, it's never too late to add to your list of parenting convictions. Be the one expert who knows what's best for your family. Refine your expertise as you disciple your children. Learn from your mistakes and keep moving ahead. Keep growing in your own relationship with God, and trust him as your ultimate parenting authority. You and God together are an unbeatable combination!

Source Notes

Introduction

[1] Interview with Oprah Winfrey on the BET network quoted in *USA Today,* May 30, 1995, 3D.
[2] Genesis 2:18.
[3] Proverbs 31:28.
[4] Luke 6:31.

Chapter 1

[1] Sandra D. Wilson, *Shame-Free Parenting* (Downers Grove, IL: Inter-Varsity Press, 1992), 67.
[2] Bruno Bettleheim, *The Good Enough Parent* (New York: Random House, 1987), 9.
[3] Ibid., 12.
[4] "Parent-Hopping Not Unusual But Hard on Everyone," Albany (NY) *Times-Union*, May 4, 1994, C-6.
[5] Jack O. and Judith K. Baliswick, *The Family: A Christian Perspective on the Contemporary Home* (Grand Rapids, MI: Baker Books, 1991), 93.
[6] Ibid.
[7] Ray Guarendi with David Eich, *Back to the Family* (New York: Simon and Schuster, 1990), 61.
[8] Benjamin Spock and Michael Rothenberg, *Baby and Child Care* (New York: Pocket Books, 1985).
[9] Bettleheim, *The Good Enough Parent*, 8.
[10] Rodney Clapp, *Families at the Crossroads* (Downers Grove, IL: Inter-Varsity Press, 1993), 49.
[11] Ibid.
[12] Guarendi with Eich, 64-5.
[13] Baliswick and Baliswick, *The Family*, 109.
[14] Dr. Arthur Cherry, quoted in Linda Lee Small, "Parents Don't Have to Be Perfect," *Working Mother*, Feb., 1991, 62, 65.
[15] Bruno Bettleheim, *The Good Enough Parent* (New York: Random House, 1987), 3.
[16] Guarendi with Eich, 61.
[17] Guarendi with Eich, 161.

[18] Robin Marantz Henig, "Are You the Parent Your Child Needs Now?," *Child*, April 1994, 95.

[19] Cherry quoted in Small, 65.

[20] David Grant, "When A Parent is Weak," *Christian Parenting Today*, Jan.-Feb. 1991, 10.

[21] Small, "Parents Don't Have to Be Perfect," 65.

[22] Gloria Chisholm, "Beyond Tough," *Christian Parenting Today*, March-April, 1994, 50.

[23] Nick Stinnett and John DeFrain, *Secrets of Strong Families*, (New York: Berkeley Books, 1986), 159.

[24] Gloria Chisholm, "Count on Me," *Christian Parenting Today*, May-June, 1994, 66.

[25] Guarendi with Eich, 109.

[26] Ibid., 108.

[27] Quoted in David Elkind, *Ties That Stress: The New Family Imbalance* (Cambridge, MA: Harvard University Press, 1994), 94.

[28] Elkind makes this argument persuasively in *Ties That Stress*, 93-100.

[29] Bruno Bettleheim, *The Good Enough Parent* (New York: Random House, 1987)

Chapter 2

[1] Linda Lee Small, "Parents Don't Have to Be Perfect," *Working Mother*, Feb., 1991, 63.

[2] Cherry quoted in Small, "Parents Don't Have to Be Perfect," 62, 65.

[3] *Parenting*, Nov., 1990, 24. (no author given)

[4] Sandra D. Wilson, *Shame-Free Parenting* (Downers Grove, IL: Inter-Varsity Press, 1992), 66.

[5] Richard Patterson, Jr., *It's The Little Things That Count,* (Nashville, TN: Thomas Nelson, 1993).

[6] Ray Guarendi with David Eich, *Back to the Family* (New York: Simon and Schuster, 1990), 87.

[7] Ibid., 88.

[8] Small, "Parents Don't Have to Be Perfect," 65.

[9] Ray Guarendi with David Eich, *Back to the Family* , 89-90.

[10] Small, "Parents Don't Have to Be Perfect," 65.

[11] 1 Corinthians 13: 4-5.

[12] Ray Guarendi with David Eich, *Back to the Family* , 35.

[13] I owe this helpful illustration to Nick Stinnett and John DeFrain, *Secrets of Strong Families*, (New York: Berkeley Books, 1986).

[14] Small, "Parents Don't Have to Be Perfect," 65.

[15] Sandra D. Wilson, *Shame Free Parenting*, 11.

[16] Ray Guarendi with David Eich, *Back to the Family* , 39-42.

[17] Ibid., 43-44.

[18] Philippians 3:13-14.

[19] David Grant, "When A Parent is Weak," *Christian Parenting Today*, Jan.-Feb. 1991, 10.

[20] Small, "Parents Don't Have to Be Perfect," 65.

[21] Rodney Clapp, *Families at the Crossroads* (Downers Grove, IL: Inter-Varsity Press, 1993), 142.

[22] Sandra D. Wilson, *Shame Free Parenting*, 200.

[23] Jonah 3:1.

[24] William Ayres, "To Teach," *Context,* Vol. 26, #9, May 1, 1995, 3.

[25] Ray Guarendi with David Eich, *Back to the Family* , 66.

[26] Ibid., 65.

[27] Kay Kuzma, "To Spank or Not To Spank," *Christian Parenting Today*, Sept.-Oct. 1991, 68.

Chapter 3

[1] Penelope Leach, "How to Make Your Child Want to be Good," *Child*, Sept., 1994, 100.

[2] "Cat's in the Cradle," Words and Music by Harry Chapin and Sandy Chapin.

[3] Elinor J. Brecher, "Parents May Fail at Task," Albany, NY, *Times-Union*, Feb. 29,1994, H-1.

[4] Ibid., H-6.

[5] Sandra D. Wilson, *Shame-Free Parenting* (Downers Grove, IL: Inter-Varsity Press, 1992), 66-67.

[6] Ray Guarendi with David Eich, *Back to the Family* (New York: Simon and Schuster, 1990), 65.

[7] Anna Quindlen, "What is a Good Child?," *Parenting*, April, 1998, 133.

[8] John S. Dacey and Alex J. Packer, *The Nurturing Parent* (New York: Simon and Schuster, 1992), 50.

[9] Quoted in Josh McDowell, "Black and White in a World Where Anything Goes," *Christian Parenting Today*, Sept./Oct., 1994, 38.

[10] Barbara J. Berg, "Learning Right from Wrong," *Parents*, March, 1990, 102.

[11] Quindlen, *Parenting*, 133.

[12] I Timothy 6:6.

[13] Deuteronomy 6: 6-9.

[14] Matthew 6:21.

[15] Jack O. and Judith K. Baliswick, *The Family: A Christian Perspective on the Contemporary Home* (Grand Rapids, MI: Baker Book House, 1991), 96-8.

[16] See Deuteronomy 6:6-7.

[17] 1 Peter 5:7.

[18] Richard Patterson, Jr., *It's The Little Things That Count,* (Nashville, TN: Thomas Nelson, 1993), 21-22.

Chapter 4

[1] Barbara Defoe Whitehead, "Dan Quayle Was Right," *Atlantic Monthly,* April, 1993, 47.

[2] Ibid.

[3] Ibid.

[4] Ibid.

[5] Ecclesiastes 4:9-10 (NRSV)

[6] Richard Louv, *FatherLove,* (New York, NY: Simon and Schuster, 1993), 186.

[7] David Blankenhorn, *Fatherless America: Confronting America's Most Urgent Social Problem,* (New York, NY: Basic Books, 1995), 67.

[8] Blankenhorn, *Fatherless America,* 2 and 67ff.

[9] Blankenhorn, *Fatherless America,* 60.

[10] Miriam Durkin, "Case for Two Parent Families Gains Momentum," Albany (NY) *Times-Union,* May 23, 1993, A-1.

[11] Blankenhorn outlines this argument and effectively critiques it in Fatherless America, chapters 4-6.

[12] David Broder, "Quayle Was Right About 1 Parent Families," Albany, NY, *Times-Union,* March 24, 1993, A-11.

[13] Richard LaLiberte, "The Daddy Bond," *Parents,* November, 1995, 101.

[14] Mitch and Susan Golant, *Finding Time For Fathering,* (New York, NY: Ballentine Books, 1992), 45.

[15] Op. Cite

[16] Mitch and Susan Golant, *Finding Time For Fathering,* 46.

[17] Susan Reimer, "Left Alone, Dads Run The Family by Other Rules," Albany (NY) *Times Union,* Oct. 1, 1993, A-9.

[18] Durkin, "Case for Two Parent Families Gains Momentum," A-1.

[19] "Parental Divorce, Adolescent Delinquency," *Family In America* (New Research) Rockford Institute, Rockford, IL, January, 1994, 2.

[20] "In The Shadow of Parental Divorce," *Family In America* (New Research) Rockford Institute, Rockford, IL, February, 1993, 1.

[21] Aaron Hass, *The Gift of Fatherhood: How Men's Lives Are Transformed by Their Children,* (New York, NY: Simon and Schuster, 1994) 28-9.

[22] Blankenhorn, *Fatherless America*, 216-17.
[23] Louv, *FatherLove*, 90-91.
[24] Hass, *The Gift of Fatherhood*, 91.
[25] Evelyn Bassoff, "Life without Father," *Parents*, October, 1995, 108.
[26] Blankenhorn, *Fatherless America*, 72.
[27] Marilyn Elias, "Studies Find Dads make Difference," *USA Today*, Aug. 24, 1998, D-1.
[28] Blankenhorn, *Fatherless America*, 81.
[29] Ibid., 78.
[30] Ibid., 82.
[31] Louv, *FatherLove*, 18.
[32] Phillipians 4: 8 (NRSV).
[33] Blankenhorn, *Fatherless America*, 218.
[34] Ibid., 219.
[35] Ibid., 45.
[36] See, for example, Ephesians 6:4.
[37] Op. Cit.
[38] Luke 6:31.
[39] Matthew. 18:2-6.
[40] Ephesians 4:29.
[41] 1 Peter 4:8.
[42] 1 Corinthians 11:1.
[43] Ecclesiastes 1:9.
[44] The Center for Parent/Youth Understanding, *Newsletter*, Summer, 1995, 1.
[45] Louv, *FatherLove*, 4.
[46] Blankenhorn, *Fatherless America*, 212.
[47] Elias, USA Today, Aug. 24, 1998, D-1.

Chapter 5

[1] Elizabeth Berg, "Little Moments That Mean A Lot," *Parents*, Sept. 1991, 78.
[2] John S. Dacey and Alex J. Packer, *The Nurturing Parent* (New York: Simon and Schuster, 1992), 77.
[3] Ray Guarendi with David Eich, *Back to the Family* (New York: Simon and Schuster, 1990),115.
[4] Penelope Leach, "What Every Child Needs," *Child*, May, 1994, 110.
[5] Ray Guarendi with David Eich, *Back to the Family* , 132.
[6] Ibid., 118.
[7] Jeanie Kasindorf, "Parents Who Can't Commit," *Child*, Sept., 1992, 98.
[8] Ibid., 129.

[9] Richard Patterson, Jr., *It's the Little Things that Count*, (Nashville, TN: Thomas Nelson, 1993), 20-21.

[10] Paul Lewis, "Taming The Lions of Fatherhood," *Christian Parenting Today*, March-April, 1992, 26.

[11] Ibid., 27.

[12] Ray Guarendi with David Eich, *Back to the Family*, 119.

[13] E. Berg, "Little Moments," *Parents*, Sept. 1991, 78-9.

[14] Lewis, "Taming The Lions of Fatherhood," 28.

[15] Ibid.

[16] Ibid.

[17] "Cat's in the Cradle" Words and Music by Harry Chapin and Sandy Chapin.

[18] Ray Guarendi with David Eich, *Back to the Family*, 43.

[19] See Kathy Henderson, "Making The Most of Quality Time," *Working Mother*, Sept., 1991 and Susan Buchsbaum, "The '90's Slowdown," *Child*, Nov., 1991 for a helpful explanation of the development of the concept of "quality time."

[20] Ray Guarendi with David Eich, *Back to the Family*, 121.

[21] Kathy Henderson, "Making The Most of Quality Time," *Working Mother*, Sept., 1991 (no page numbers given).

[22] Ray Guarendi with David Eich, *Back to the Family*, 120.

[23] Susan Buchsbaum, "The '90's Slowdown," *Child*, Nov., 1991, 72.

[24] Ray Guarendi with David Eich, *Back to the Family*, 121.

[25] Penelope Leach, "Are You Dad Enough?," *Parenting,* Oct., 1992, 91.

[26] Susan Buchsbaum, "The '90's Slowdown," *Child*, Nov., 1991, 72.

[27] Ray Guarendi with David Eich, *Back to the Family*, 121.

[28] Penelope Leach, "What Every Child Needs," 110.

[29] Buchsbaum, "The '90's Slowdown," 72.

[30] Ibid.

[31] Ava Siegler, "Redefining Quality Time," *Child*, May, 1994, 40.

[32] Linda Seaver in Kasindorf, "Parents Who Can't Commit," 92.

[33] Penelope Leach, "Are You Dad Enough?," 88.

[34] Bettye Caldwell, "Have Fun With Your Toddler," *Working Mother*, Nov., 1993, 70.

[35] Ray Guarendi with David Eich, *Back to the Family*, 123.

Chapter 6

[1] Luke 6:31.

[2] Matthew 18:1-6, Mark 10: 13-16.

[3] "Dr. Dobson Answers Your Questions," *Focus on the Family* Magazine, Feb., 1995, 5.

[4] Bernice Weissbourd, "Discipline with Respect," *Parents*, Feb., 1995, 74.

[5] Jo Ann Larsen, "Lighten Up!," *Working Mother*, November, 1994, 53.

[6] Ibid.

[7] Ibid.

[8] Collen Plakut in "Your Ideas," *Parents*, Feb., 1995, 16.

[9] Dr. James Dobson, "Successful Discipline," *Focus on the Family Bulletin*, January, 1995.

[10] Ibid.

[11] Anne Cassidy, "Rites of Privacy," *Parenting*, November, 1994, 122.

[12] Ibid., 125.

[13] Ibid., 128.

[14] Ibid.

[15] Ephesians 4:29.

[16] Ray Guarendi with David Eich, *Back to the Family* (New York: Simon and Schuster, 1990).

[17] Ibid., 235-39.

[18] Ibid., 239-41.

[19] Lisa Collier Cool, "Loving Limits," *Child*, January, 1991, 104. She reports on a 20 year study of three discipline styles by Dr. Diana Baumrind, University of California at Berkeley.

[20] Jack O. and Judith K. Baliswick, *The Family: A Christian Perspective on the Contemporary Home* (Grand Rapids, MI: Baker Book House, 1991), 101.

[21] Ray Guarendi with David Eich, *Back to the Family*, 154.

[22] Ibid.

[23] Ibid., 152.

[24] Ibid., 155.

[25] Baliswick and Baliswick, *The Family*, 95-96.

[26] Ibid.

[27] Ibid., 100-01.

[28] Penelope Leach, "Instead of Spanking," *Parenting*, Dec./Jan., 1992, 230.

[29] Baliswick and Baliswick, *The Family*, 102.

Chapter 7

[1] Source unknown.

[2] Penelope Leach, "Instead of Spanking," *Parenting*, Dec./Jan., 1992, 89.

[3] Ibid.

[4] This section distinguishing discipline and punishments relies on David Grant, "Corrective Measures," *Christian Parenting Today*, July-August, 1991, 11.

[5] Leach, "Instead of Spanking," 89.

[6] Jay Kessler, *Raising Responsible Kids*, (Brentwood, TN: Wolgemuth and Hyatt, 1991). 91.

[7] Ibid., 94.

[8] Jack O. and Judith K. Baliswick, *The Family: A Christian Perspective on the Contemporary Home* (Grand Rapids, MI: Baker Book House, 1991), 103.

[9] Kessler, *Raising Responsible Kids*, 98.

[10] Ibid.

[11] Richard Patterson, Jr., *It's The Little Things That Count,* (Nashville, TN: Thomas Nelson, 1993), Chapters 5, 6.

[12] Kessler, *Raising Responsible Kids*, 95.

[13] Ibid., 99-100.

[14] Baliswick and Baliswick, *The Family,* 94.

[15] Ray Guarendi with David Eich, *Back to the Family* (New York: Simon and Schuster, 1990), 250.

[16] Ibid.

[17] Ibid.

[18] Roger Allen and Ron Rose, *Common Sense Discipline*, (Waco, TX: Word, Inc., 1986), 24.

[19] Source unknown.

[20] Bernice Weissbourd, "Discipline with Respect," *Parents*, Feb., 1995, 74.

[21] Baliswick and Baliswick, *The Family,* 98.

[22] Kevin Lehman, "What Makes a Functional Family?," *Focus on the Family* magazine, Feb., 1995, 13.

[23] Ibid.

[24] Guarendi with Eich, *Back to the Family,* 250.

[25] Joan Wester Anderson, "Secret Rewards of Listening," *Christian Parenting Today*, Jan.-Feb., 1993, 48.

[26] Guarendi with Eich, *Back to the Family,* 141.

[27] John S. Dacey and Alex J. Packer, *The Nurturing Parent* (New York: Simon and Schuster, 1992), 35.

[28] Proverbs 18:13.

[29] Guarendi with Eich, *Back to the Family,* 142.

[30] Op. Cite

[31] Guarendi with Eich, *Back to the Family,* 161.

[32] Dacey and Packer, *The Nurturing Parent*, 21.

[33] Quoted in ibid., 22.

[34] Diane Hales, "Lighten Up and Enjoy Your Family More," *Working Mother*, Nov., 1994, 55.

[35] Tamara Eberlein, "The Ten Worst Discipline Mistakes Parents Make," *Redbook*, June, 1993, 176.

[36] Ibid., 172.

[37] Allen and Rose, *Common Sense Discipline*, 58.
[38] Kessler, *Raising Responsible Kids*, 57.
[39] Dacey and Packer, *The Nurturing Parent*, 37.
[40] Guarendi with Eich, *Back to the Family*, 161.
[41] Jane Nelson, *Positive Discipline,* (New York, NY: Ballantine Books, 1981), 68-78.
[42] Leach, "Instead of Spanking," 230.
[43] Dacey and Packer, *The Nurturing Parent*, 49.
[44] Dr. James Dobson, "Successful Discipline" in *Focus on the Family Bulletin*, January, 1995.
[45] Dr. James Dobson, "A Sample 'Focus on the Family' Commentary," *Focus on the Family* magazine, December, 1995, 13.
[46] Dacey and Packer, *The Nurturing Parent,* 17.
[47] Hales, "Lighten Up," 55.
[48] Dacey and Packer, *The Nurturing Parent*, 33-4.
[49] Ibid., 49.
[50] Leach, "Instead of Spanking," 230.
[51] Tom Peters, "Peters on Excellence," Albany, NY, *Times-Union*, Jan. 25, 1995, D-3.
[52] Kessler, *Raising Responsible Kids*, 46.
[53] Luke 15:11-32.
[54] Baliswick and Baliswick, *The Family,* 129.
[55] Ibid., 131.
[56] Lehman, "What Makes a Functional Family?, 13.
[57] Leach, "Instead of Spanking," 230.

Chapter 8

[1] Dr. J. Gelles quoted in Mary C. Hickey, "To Spank Or Not To Spank," *Working Mother*, Jan., 1991, 48.
[2] Den A. Trumball, M.D. and S. DuBose Ravenel, M.D., "Spare the Rod: New Research Challenges Spanking Critics," *Family Policy*, Vol.9 No.5, 1996, 2.
[3] Op Cit.
[4] Proverbs 13:24.
[5] Proverbs 23:13.
[6] Proverbs 22:15.
[7] John Rosemond, *To Spank Or Not To Spank: A Parents' Handbook,* (Kansas City, MO: Andrews and McMeel, 1994), 37.
[8] Ibid.
[9] See Isaiah 28:27.
[10] Rosemond, *To Spank Or Not To Spank*, 37.

[11] Jack O. and Judith K. Baliswick, *The Family: A Christian Perspective on the Contemporary Home* (Grand Rapids, MI: Baker Book House, 1991), 98.

[12] Proverbs 22:6.

[13] Rosemond, *To Spank Or Not To Spank*, 38.

[14] Baliswick and Baliswick, *The Family,* 98.

[15] Trumball and Ravenel, "Spare the Rod," 7.

[16] Rosemond, *To Spank Or Not To Spank*, 14.

[17] Ibid., 49-50.

[18] Kay Kuzma, "To Spank Or Not To Spank," *Christian Parenting Today*, Sept.-Oct., 1991, 66.

[19] Rosemond, *To Spank Or Not To Spank*, 40.

[20] Ibid., 63, 46.

[21] Trumball and Ravenel, 7.

[22] Kuzma, 68.

[23] Nancy Samalin with Catherine Whitney, "What's Wrong With Spanking?" *Parents*, May, 1995, 36.

[24] Roger Allen and Ron Rose, *Common Sense Discipline*, (Waco, TX: Word, Inc., 1986), 35.

[25] Rosemond, *To Spank Or Not To Spank*, 50-51.

[26] Kuzma, 66.

[27] William and Martha Sears, "Positively No!," *Christian Parenting Today*, Feb., 1995, 89.

[28] Den A. Trumball and S. DuBose Ravenel, "To Spank or not to Spank?" *Focus on the Family* Magazine, April, 1998, 4.

[29] Ibid., 7.

[30] Rosemond, *To Spank Or Not To Spank*, 41.

[31] Trumball and Ravenel, "Spare the Rod," 7.

[32] Ibid.

[33] Samalin with Whitney, "What's Wrong With Spanking?" 36.

[34] Hickey, "To Spank Or Not To Spank," 49.

[35] Ibid.

[36] Rosemond, *To Spank Or Not To Spank,* 8. See Also Trumball and Ravenell, "Spare the Rod."

[37] Trumball and Ravenel, "Spare the Rod," 7.

[38] Mitch and Susan Golant, "The Truth about Consequences," *Child*, Nov., 1991, 105.

[39] Rudolf Dreikurs, *Children: The Challenge,* (New York, NY: Hawthorn/ Dutton, 1964).

[40] Ibid., 76.

[41] Ibid., 79.

[42] Ibid., 84-5.

[43] Jane Nelson, *Positive Discipline,* (New York, NY: Ballantine Books, 1981), 13.

[44] Baliswick and Baliswick, *The Family,* 129.

[45] Op. Cite, 73.

[46] Ray Guarendi with David Eich, *Back to the Family* (New York: Simon and Schuster, 1990), 250.

[47] Ibid.

[48] Dena K. Salmon, "Making Time Outs Work," *Parents,* Feb., 1992, 98.

[49] Penelope Leach, "Instead of Spanking," *Parenting,* Dec./Jan., 1992, 92.

[50] Op. Cite

[51] Jacqueline Mitchard, "Time Outs: Should You or Shouldn't You?," *Parenting,* Oct., 1994, 71.

[52] Salmon, "Making Time Outs Work," 102.

[53] Ibid., 98.

[54] Ibid., 102.

[55] Dr. Steven J. Bavolek in Salmon, "Making Time Outs Work," 102.

[56] Ibid.

[57] Lisa Collier Cool, "Loving Limits," *Child,* Nov., 1991, 106.

[58] Salmon, "Making Time Outs Work," 98.

[59] Ibid.

[60] I rely heavily in this section on the excellent article by Helen Harpham, "Don't Forget the Mercy," *Christian Parenting Today,* Nov.-Dec., 1989.

[61] Ibid., 63.

[62] Ibid., 64.

[63] Ibid., 64.

Chapter 9

[1] John Rosemond, "Parents Can Just Say 'No' to Their Kids," Albany (NY) *Times-Union,* Sept. 8, 1995, C-1.

[2] Ray Guarendi with David Eich, *Back to the Family* (New York: Simon and Schuster, 1990), 249.

[3] Ibid.

[4] Guarendi with Eich, *Back to the Family,* 248.

[5] Richard Louv, *FatherLove,* (New York, NY: Simon and Schuster, 1993), 186.

[6] Alice E. Chase quoted in "Dear Abby," Albany (NY) *Times-Union,* August 25, 1995, D-2.

[7] Josh McDowell, "Black and White in a World Where Anything Goes," *Christian Parenting Today,* Sept.-Oct. 1994, 40.

[8] James 1:5.

[9] See Genesis 4:1-8 and Luke 13:11-32

[10] Proverbs 22:6.

[11] Mary Manz Simon, "No Warranty Included," *Christian Parenting Today,* Sept.-Oct. 1994, 22.

[12] Psalms 138:8.

[13] Jeremiah 29:11.

For information about this and other Tekna
Books titles, please visit our website.

www.teknabooks.com

TEKNA BOOKS™
Publishing for our Future